Colin Thomas Flahive has been living and traveling in China for more than 16 years. He currently lives with his wife in Kunming, where, in addition to writing, he runs multiple businesses and social enterprises.

In *Great Leaps,* Colin explores China's rural-urban migration against the backdrop of his own transition from Colorado to southwest China. There he partnered with three friends to open a café that became much more than simply an outpost of Western cuisine in a far-flung corner of the world.

Over the course of a decade, Salvador's Coffee House became home to more than fifty young women from mountain villages in the surrounding countryside. Most knew nothing about coffee or Western food, but they moved to the city to work at Salvador's and earn their independence.

Great Leaps follows the challenges faced by Colin, his partners and his employees as they leave their old lives behind to make a new home in a foreign land. They encounter unlikely successes, endure heartbreaks and nearly lose everything. But by taking the leap together, they all find their own places in the modern Chinese dream.

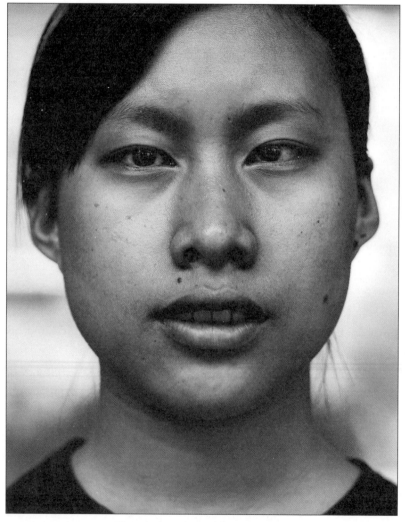

Yaya – photo by Stephan Schacher

GREAT LEAPS

*Finding home in
a changing China*

Colin Thomas Flahive

BLACKSMITH BOOKS

Great Leaps: Finding home in a changing China

ISBN 978-988-79638-0-6

Published by Blacksmith Books
Unit 26, 19/F, Block B, Wah Lok Industrial Centre,
37-41 Shan Mei Street, Fo Tan, Hong Kong
Tel: (+852) 2877 7899
www.blacksmithbooks.com

Edited by Paul Christensen
Maps by Matthew Hartzell

Author's acknowledgements: Thanks to everyone who proved that writing doesn't have to be such a lonesome process. Special thanks to Ryan, Mom, Dad, Roshana, Denise, Cass, Chris, Chris, Kris, Naoko, Josh, John, John, Pat, Pat, Dena, Lisa, Dan, Elliott, Matt, Matt, Matthew, Annette, Wang Hu, Zhang Yunbin, Yaya and the rest of the Salvador's staff.

Contents

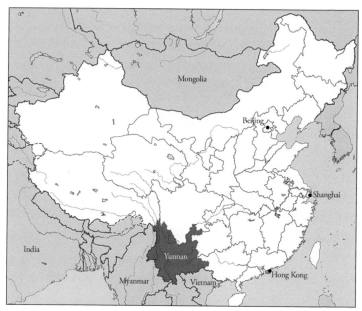

Maps of China (above) and Yunnan Province (below)

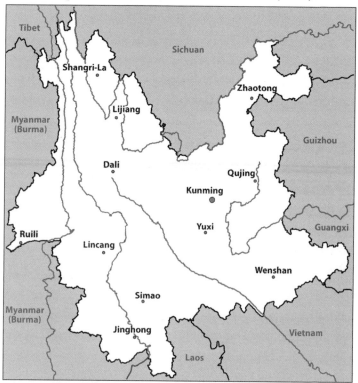

Foreword

Walking across Green Lake Park in Yunnan's capital city of Kunming on the morning of Christmas Eve in 2008, I was struck by the deep azure perfection of the cloudless sky above. As I made my way past the park's large willow trees and bamboo groves in just a t-shirt, the sun warmed my skin as a cool breeze gently lilted. Old people exercised and played music. Children ran around and laughed.

I was living the dream, or at least my dream: riding the wave of China's opening up to the world in a big city with a pleasant climate, clean air and lots of other dreamers. Normally on such a beautiful day – and Kunming has a lot of beautiful days – I wouldn't be in such a hurry. But my pleasant park surroundings belied the sick churning I felt inside.

A few minutes earlier, I had been jarred out of my dream by a phone call that I'd always secretly dreaded.

"Hey…" my friend said on the other end of the line, "did you hear about Sal's?"

I knew instantly from the tone of his voice that something very bad had happened at the café where I'd hung out almost every day for the previous four years. He was short on details, but did mention the word "bomb". I headed straight out the door.

Making haste to get to the scene of the bombing, I began thinking of a Kunming without Sal's and simply couldn't imagine it. Sal's was where I'd made dozens of good friends – both locals and expats. It was a place that made living in Kunming during those years one of the happiest times of my life. Its owners and employees were all my friends, and I was intensely worried about their safety.

Arriving at Sal's, I saw the place that I jokingly referred to as my 'living room' in a cold and unfamiliar light. It was crawling with police and cordoned off from the public. A crowd had gathered outside the cordon and people were chattering about what had happened. Minutes later I got a call through to my friend Colin, one of the four owners. He was at the police station and sounded shaken, but he managed to utter exactly what I wanted to hear him say at that moment: "Everyone's OK."

*   *   *

It was a late Friday afternoon four years earlier in the summer of 2004 when I first climbed onto a bar stool at Salvador's Coffee House. The day before, I'd finished my last day as an overworked editor at a publishing company in Shanghai.

And there I was, halfway across China, sitting at a big wooden bar a few steps above Wenhua Xiang, one of the cooler little lanes in Kunming's university district . My timing was good. It just so happened that that particular Friday was the opening day for Salvador's first location in my favorite Chinese city.

It didn't take long for me to start questioning my plan to return to Shanghai after a month's vacation to search for another soul-destroying desk job. By the time I was on my second drink, I'd already decided that I was going to move to Kunming. I also knew that Salvador's would be both my second office and hangout joint of choice.

It was an easy sell. I looked at myself: pasty white, run down, unaccustomed to smiling and sporting some serious panda eyes from working 60ish hours a week. I looked well older than my 27 years.

I felt like the odd man out at that night's opening party as I met many people who are still my good friends today. Everyone seemed to be tanned, smiling and glowing. The Chinese I met were friendly and welcoming. Most of the foreigners could speak decent Chinese, and many were fluent. Nobody was exchanging business cards. The sound of laughter was everywhere. I felt at home for the first time in years. I decided that I'd rather be poor in Kunming than rolling in cash in Shanghai. At least I knew where to get good coffee and bagels.

I made the move, and for the next eight-plus years I probably averaged more than one trip a day to Sal's, as the growing number of regulars called it. For me it served many functions beyond providing coffee, food and booze. I had countless useful conversations with the four owners, getting to know all of them better than I had in Dali, where I'd met them all years before. I spoke with Colin about off-the-beaten-path travel spots in other parts of the province. Josh and I discussed different business ideas, some more crackpot than others. When he wasn't practicing his juggling or passing me shots of whiskey in teacups, Kris gave me useful help on where to get things around town. Naoko helped me better understand Chinese medicine and the local bureaucracy. All four of them were ready to lend me an ear during the many moments of self-doubt I experienced while trying to make things work in a city that even most coastal Chinese thought of as far-off and exotic.

After I'd settled into the chilled-out, sun-drenched Kunming lifestyle, the idea of moving back to smoggy and congested Shanghai or any other big Chinese city was out of the question. Life was an adventure rather than a routine. It was easy to smile, and I laughed more than I had in years. The whole city felt like a promising startup company that was just beginning to get traction, and for me Sal's was an apt symbol of what was going on in a city that was far behind Shanghai in opening up to the world – but whose day had come.

By the time Sal's opened in Kunming it already had a crew of reliable staff that had come over from the original location in Dali. They were from an impoverished area near China's border with Myanmar, a region I never visited until the wedding that opens this book. To them, I was basically a Martian. In the beginning I found it difficult understanding most of the girls' Chinese, which, if not speaking a minority language, was usually a mix of Mandarin and the Yunnan dialect, often with a heavy regional accent. But we would gradually get to know each other, especially over the large 'family dinners' they cooked in the restaurant's first year, when business was much slower than today. They would tell me tales of their remote villages and I would try to explain the American suburbs from which I came. Eventually we were cracking jokes in each others' languages and I began to think of them as my meimei, or younger sisters, despite our very different backgrounds.

After I'd blown all my savings from Shanghai on a year's rent, a nice new mountain bike and a bit of travel, I had to find a job. Other than teaching English, which I didn't particularly enjoy, there weren't really any jobs for me. Kunming wasn't fully plugged into the global economy at that point, and I quickly realized that I'd have to create my own job. I decided to build a website that was an online version of what Sal's was for me and many others – a place where people can connect with each other and learn what was happening in this increasingly buzzing blue-skied city where the ubiquitous rhythms of demolition and construction were punctuated by car horns, chirping birds or the singing advertisement of the man who sharpens knives blasting on loop from a crackly bullhorn.

Broke and frustrated with my website that nobody knew existed, I caught my first big break when I somehow convinced the owners of Sal's to do a food-for-advertising barter deal with me. In retrospect, I don't know how convincing my sales pitch was, they probably just didn't want me to starve.

Suddenly, with my food and caffeine requirements covered (I still had to pay for booze – they weren't fools), I was able to put more effort into my website. Things started coming together, and I frequently met with interview subjects or potential advertisers at Sal's. Life was getting better for everyone, and it was hard not to feel genuinely optimistic about the future.

The bombing of Salvador's shook everyone. It snapped me out of my happy daze and reminded me that nothing should be taken for granted. It also made me take stock of my life and find a new appreciation for the wonderful people I bumped into at the same places every day.

When Sal's reopened, it was a heavy but cathartic moment, a statement that just as before, everybody present refused to live their lives in fear. We moved forward together, all a little bit closer than before. We overheard, but ignored, the passersby who would point and say words like 'bombing' or 'terrorism'. After a year, the rest of the city seemed to forget about what had happened – the city was developing at a dizzying pace and had little time to dwell on the past.

I spent another four years in Kunming, during which the time came for me to sell the website, pack up and seek new challenges in Hong Kong. My last breakfast as a Kunming resident was, of course, at Salvador's. Colin and Josh were there to see me off. None of us spoke much. We'd said everything that needed saying over the past eight-and-a-half years. I was holding myself together fairly well until I grabbed my bags and began to walk away from Sal's. I began to sob, despite my efforts to put on a brave face. As a foreigner living in Kunming, Sal's meant more to me than burritos and beers. It was the one place that felt like it was home, and many of the people I'd met there were like family to me.

*   *   *

This book is much more than just one American's story about his experiences in a random corner of China. It's a close-up shot of one of the biggest things to happen to the world in the past decade, in which the template for the economic boom that had dramatically re-made Beijing, Shanghai and Guangzhou was rolled out to the rest of the world's most populous country.

This wave of wealth generation set a lot of different trends in motion. Among them was the movement of both poor rural Chinese and young foreigners toward China's lesser-known cities in search of opportunity – and adventure.

Salvador's Coffee House was one of the many places in China where these vastly different worlds collided, resulting in no shortage cross-cultural wackiness, lifelong friendships and even a few marriages and families.

My Kunming days may be behind me, but every day I'm reminded of my time there. Much of who I am today was shaped by the years I spent as a dreamer floating among a sea of dreamers at a tiny café in a forgotten part of the world. For that I will forever be grateful.

Chris Horton

Pronunciation Guide

There is nothing like a mispronounced Chinese name to make a sinophile cringe. You may think you know your *Wongs* and *Wangs*, but you've likely got them both wrong. Even though you may be saying *Wong* correctly, as in *wrong* without the "r," the accepted modern spelling in standard Mandarin is actually *Wang*. And as for the way you've been pronouncing *Wang* in the past, know that the Chinese language actually has no "ang" sound as we would pronounce in the word *clang*.

Pinyin is now the most accepted system of spelling out Chinese syllables with the Roman alphabet, but most non-sinophiles find the relation between spelling and pronunciation challenging.

Two of the more counter-intuitive pronunciations in Pinyin are for "q" and "x." Like in the word *qi*, "q" actually has a "ch" sound. "X," on the other hand, has a "sh" sound so that *xi* sounds like *she*. With this in mind, below are some of the names and places in the following story so that you don't stumble when you encounter them.

The pronunciation for the first two names, *Yaya* and *A Li* hold no big surprises. *Yaya* means "sprout" and *A Li* is pronounced just like the name *Ali*.

Zhou is one of the most popular family names in China. "Zh" has a sound similar to "j" so that *Zhou* is pronounced just like *Joe*.

Shifu is pronounced like *shirt*, without the "t," plus "fu" like in *kungfu*.

The first syllable in *Rongjie* sounds like *wrong* with the "o" pronounced as it is in *boat*. The second syllable has a "j" sound combined with what *yes* would sound like without the "s." *Wrōng J-ye*.

Mengjuan also has two syllables. The first one combines an "m" with the "ung" sound in *sung*. The second syllable has a "j" combined with the "wen" sound in *went*. *M-ung J-wen*.

The first syllable in *Lincang* sounds like the word *lean*. The second syllable combines the "ts" sound in *cats* with the "ong" sound in song. *Lean Ts-ong*.

Don't make the same mistake when pronouncing *Bangdong* as you used to make with *Wang* and *Wong*. *Bang* in Pinyin is actually pronounced like we say *bong*. *Dong* is pronounced similarly to how your instinct tells you but with the "o" having a sound like it does in *boat*. *Bong Dōng*.

Wang Hu and *Zhang Yunbin* are not as hard to pronounce as they might look. You have already learned to say *Wang* correctly and *Hu* is pretty much pronounced the same as we say "who." Like in *Zhou*, the "zh" sound in *Zhang* is similar to "j," while the "ang" part sounds like "ong" as in song. *Yunbin* is two syllables with *yun* sounding like *you* with an "n" thrown on the end and *bin* sounding similar to *been*, as in, "where have you *been?*" *Wong who, J-ong You-n Been*.

Qin Hui combines a "ch" sound with the "ean" sound in *clean* plus the sound you would get by attaching an "h" in front of *way*. *Ch-ean H-way*.

Aling is pronounced pretty much like you might guess with the first syllable sounding like a satisfied "ah" sound and the second syllable sounding like *bling* without the "b." *Ah Ling*.

The first syllable in *Xiao Hua*'s name sounds like *she* combined with a painful, "ow." Be sure to pronounce it as one syllable, "she-ow." The second syllable, *hua*, means "flower," and is pronounced as "hwa." *She-owe Hwa*.

Xuanwei might take some practice. Start with the first syllable by trying to combine the "sh" in *she* with the "wen" in *went*. *Wei* is pronounced just like we say *way*. *Sh-wen Way*.

By now you should be able to guess how to pronounce *Zhuhong*. *Zhu* has the same pronunciation as we say *Jew*, and *hong* combines an "h" sound with the "ong" in *song* but with the "o" having the same sound as in *boat*. *Jew H-ōng*.

Dollars mentioned in the text refer to US dollars.

We must walk consciously
only part way toward our goal,
and then leap in the dark
to our success.

Henry David Thoreau

CHAPTER I

FROM THE COUNTRYSIDE

Yaya took nothing with her but a warm jacket, a toothbrush and a washcloth all bundled together in a tattered white shopping bag. It was the first time that she'd ever left her village and she looked nervous and afraid as she hiked down the dirt trail away from the only home she'd ever known.

It was a two-hour hike down the mountainside to the town of Moulan at the bottom of the valley. Moulan was already as far as she had ever been from her family, and that night, for the first time in her 17-year life, she would spend the night somewhere other than in her mountaintop village.

Her face was dark, tanned from years of working the family's tea fields, and one might have thought she was much older if not for her timid and anxious eyes. She didn't say a word to anyone as she hiked along the winding trail between terraced tea and corn fields where many of the villagers were out tending their crops. A warm wind rustled through drying corn stalks left over from the autumn harvest, making the air smell sweet.

I felt guilty. We were the reason Yaya was leaving her life in the countryside for Kunming, the largest city in China's Yunnan Province. My partners Josh, Naoko, Kris and I had started Salvador's Coffee House as a small business. It was not our intent to split up a family and take away their only child for the sake of employment. Yaya had never seen a foreigner before, never tasted coffee and had no idea how to prepare

Western food, but she would move to Kunming to work with us and she would learn.

We came to the village of Dalubian in southwest Yunnan with no intention of scouting out potential employees. We were there to attend the wedding of A Li, Salvador's manager. The entire Salvador's staff and a few friends made the 14-hour bus and tractor trip to join A Li and her family in their village. For three days we stuffed ourselves on fried pork, aged ham, pork fat-fried vegetables and stewed pork ribs – a pig had been slaughtered for the event and provided most of the occasion's cuisine.

A Li's family home was on a steep slope with terraces of tea, rice, corn and vegetables. Two wooden structures, separated by a concrete courtyard, housed the bedrooms and kitchen. The walls inside every room were plastered with old newspapers, serving as both a form of decoration and as a way to protect the old wood from stains and wear. Small steel bowls filled with stacks of burning charcoal were placed in the center of each room to keep us warm.

Water buffalo trudged along narrow dirt paths outside the house, some on their way home with their masters and some on the way to the fields to plow new rows for seeding. The distinct aroma of freshly turned manure wafted about.

The family's donkey had been put into his pen and did not seem very happy about it. Every so often he would launch into a long bray of hees and haws. Soon his friends, locked in pens in other households, were answering his call. The valley was filled with their song, sounding like a chorus of rusty seesaws.

A Li's parents had prepared their courtyard with 20 tables, each surrounded by eight stools, in order to feed more than 900 people from Dalubian and surrounding villages to celebrate their daughter's marriage. Every table would be seated about six different times that day in order to make sure everyone was fed. The cooks in the kitchen continually stoked the wood stove and worked feverishly to get the food out quickly.

Giant bowls of steaming rice, along with slow-cooked chicken soup with ginger, fried pork fat nuggets, boiled pork balls, sliced salted pork belly, fish with pickled chili peppers and wild forest mushrooms came out of the tiny kitchen at a pace faster than any hotel buffet. There were even some special vegetable dishes cooked without pork fat for Josh and Naoko, both vegetarians. As families awaited their turn at the tables, a small group of chickens and two small dogs made sure that none of the food that fell to the ground was wasted.

The men of the village pressured us to drink shots of homemade corn liquor, a strong alcohol that Josh, Kris and I had learned to appreciate after years of living in China, but most other outsiders found revolting. Everyone welcomed A Li's husband into the family while we sang songs we didn't know the lyrics to and danced as the family's donkey looked on bitterly. At the end of it all, Yaya slowly made her way down the mountain with her tattered white shopping bag.

It wasn't the first time a village girl had left her family to come work for us. Yaya would be the 33rd teenage girl to leave her village to work at Salvador's. This time, however, was different. Usually, we first met the girls in Kunming after they'd been referred to us by friends and family members of other workers. This was the first time we were there to actually witness a girl's departure from home.

There were no goodbyes, at least none that we saw. Yaya's parents stood quietly saying nothing. It wasn't that they didn't care for their daughter or wouldn't miss her, but public displays of that sort were reserved for arguments or funerals. This was a time for celebration, and Yaya and her parents would not let their emotions turn into an exhibition of affection or loss.

Yaya had an opportunity that her parents never had – to move to the city and be a part of China's modern society. Rural youths who find work in the city can provide a supplemental income for their family, sometimes even for the entire village. Teenage migrant workers often send large portions of their wages back to their parents, who then reinvest the money into seed, livestock, home improvement and medical expenses.

For most of the villagers in Dalubian and throughout rural China, moving to the city is an unrealistic ambition. The move is expensive, good work is hard to find and abandoning the farm means risking the family's only guaranteed income. Moreover, migrants from the countryside to the city are often treated poorly and discriminated against by urbanites who refer to them as *tubaozi*, or "dirt dumplings," a derogatory term for country folk similar in connotation to "country bumpkins."

China's urban migration, now the largest in the history of the world, is fueled by the idea that, regardless of birthplace or social class, cities offer everyone a chance at success. It's an idea tantamount to that of the American Dream – that people can start with nothing but succeed through hard work alone. Some might argue that in today's global climate the American Dream is dead, but for hundreds of millions in China a similar dream lives on.

Rural Chinese are nearly 50 percent of China's total population, a number that was closer to 80 percent only 30 years ago. Many of China's rural villages are hundreds, sometimes thousands of years old. When traveling through Yunnan Province you will often pass through villages that have remained relatively unchanged for centuries. Peoples' livelihoods revolve around caring for pigs, chickens, ducks, cows and sheep. They tend fields of rice, corn and wheat and collect wild mushrooms and other forest foods. They grow tea, coffee, tobacco and fruit. In the village, life is work. For many of them, the only experience of modern China comes from television.

Most outsiders, including many urban Chinese, never experience this side of China. I frequently meet tourists who say that they've traveled all over the country. They often go on to explain that they've been to Shanghai, Hong Kong, the Great Wall in Beijing, the Terracotta Warriors in Xi'an and the pandas in Chengdu. I usually just nod in agreement that, yes, they have seen *all* of China. But I can't help but think they have missed out on everything that is the China I have come to know and love. The China where meals pull families back together each evening and there's always extra just in case someone else happens to stop by. Where people cook for the pigs before cooking for the family. Where the proud clucks of a hen that just laid an egg don't go unnoticed by the hen's owner.

Where children don't practice the violin for five hours a day. Where the only traffic is a herd of goats and the only honking comes from geese. Where a walk to the neighbors' house might take a couple of hours. And where even with barking dogs, clanging cow bells, early rooster calls and roaring tractor motors, you somehow sleep more soundly than you have in a long time.

The countryside is the heart of China. The country's popular cities or historical sites will only reveal the outer layers of a much more complicated culture and society. The core of the country exists in modest homes near rice paddies, along twisting mountain trails, next to small rivers and streams and in deserts and high plateaus. There are nearly a million villages in China – home to over 700 million villagers – and it is in these villages that Chinese tradition is more than just a show for cameras, it is simply the way of life.

Yaya grew up in Dalubian, a village far removed from the modern urban China that we often read about. While urban girls her age went to school, shopped and joined internet chat rooms, she tended her family's tea, corn and rice fields and fed the pigs, cows and chickens. While urban girls were getting their nails done, Yaya's hands grew strong and calloused. Her family labored long hours to earn an income of about $50 per month from their tea and walnut trees, but they also raised all of their own food. So although Yaya worked hard, she ate well.

The elementary school in Dalubian was a half-hour walk from home, but the nearest high school was over two and a half hours away. So Yaya, along with most others in her village, never planned to attend high school. Instead, she aspired to find work somewhere outside of the village – somewhere where she could make enough money to send cash home to her mother and father. She hoped that perhaps one day she could build them a new home.

When Yaya's mother was only three months old, she fell into a fire that disfigured her hands and half of her face. Villagers in Dalubian depend on the ability to harvest crops and pick tea leaves in the fields. The permanent damage the fire had done to her hands made this kind of work nearly impossible. She was eventually married to a man who was mostly deaf – it is village tradition to pair up handicapped men and women. Most men from Yaya's village found work in construction, but such opportunities were not available for the deaf. So as a young girl with two handicapped parents, Yaya had to take on much of the workload. The day she left her village to work at Salvador's was more than just an opportunity for her. It was an opportunity for her family.

After A Li's wedding, we hiked with Yaya down the mountainside to where our driver awaited us. She was silent and visibly nervous as she stepped onto the bus destined for her new life in Kunming. I thought back to the day when I took my first trip across the Pacific from the U.S. to China. I remembered how nervous I was and how I had no idea what to expect. I could only imagine how Yaya felt. In a way, my transition to China was easier than Yaya's to Kunming. For her, Kunming was a more foreign place than it was for me. I at least understood how cities worked, but for her there was no such familiarity.

Like me, she would be considered an outsider by those from the city. But unlike me, she was just another farm girl coming to the city to look for work, looked down on by urbanites for lacking culture and education.

Josh, Naoko, Kris and I had also moved far away from our homes in the U.S. and Japan in search of something more. We left everything behind to move halfway around the world, eventually found each other, and went into business together. With Salvador's Coffee House we found our place in Kunming. We could only hope that with us, Yaya would find hers too.

We knew that our responsibility for Yaya and the rest of our employees went beyond simply providing a fair salary with safe working conditions. Salvador's was a bridge to their new futures and an opportunity for success in the city.

Two years after Yaya left her village to work at Salvador's, nearly 10 years after the four of us left the U.S. for China, Josh, Kris and I returned to meet with Yaya's parents. We sipped on tea and munched on hemp seeds, a local snack, while talking up Yaya's accomplishments at Salvador's since leaving the village. The small courtyard of Yaya's family home was nearest the top of the hill in her village and overlooked a wide valley. Hillside steps were carved into terraced plots of corn and tea and lined with walnut groves. We could see plumes of smoke rising from the valley floor as farmers cleared space for new crops by burning the old ones.

Yaya's mother brought out a big plate of peanuts and sunflower seeds. As we took in our surroundings we were surprised to discover a newly tiled house with a separate kitchen and another house extension that appeared to be under construction. This was a costly undertaking for any village family, let alone one with two disabled parents.

Yaya's mother, noticing our curious looks, pointed her scarred finger toward the new house. Proudly, she said, "Yaya built this."

CHAPTER 2

SHARKS AND MARGARITAS

"If a shark attacks you, punch it in the nose!"

I was pretty certain I'd heard that before on a nature documentary – or was I mistaken? Was it gouge the eyes or punch the nose?

Maybe any fighting chance was just a myth meant to keep people calm in the face of death, like how putting your head between your knees will somehow keep you safe in a plane crash.

I needed to choose some course of action, and quickly, because a meter-and-a-half shark was swimming circles around me in a desolate coral reef out in the Andaman Sea.

No one knew that I'd come to the island nature reserve off of Thailand's southwest coast. I'd pitched my tent on the beach, so surely someone would find my belongings if I disappeared. But my passport was tied to my waist in a waterproof bag, so there would be no easy way of identifying me. "If this shark decides to take a bite, it's possible no one will ever know where I disappeared to," I thought to myself.

The snorkel impeded each breath as panic made my respiration fast and shallow. The last thing I wanted to do was take my eyes off the animal by breaching the water to remove my snorkel, so I forced myself to try to remain calm by taking lengthy breaths. The shark's long, muscular body barely flexed with each sideways paddle of its tall tail. The shimmering silver skin was hypnotic, but I stayed focused on its eyes. The shark continued to circle me as I trod water bracing for its attack. "Just punch it in the nose," I kept thinking.

The entire point of my trip to the beach had been to recover from the malaria I'd contracted in Kolkata, India. The illness had completely drained me, and I felt I deserved some tranquil time on the beach with nothing to do but admire the corals and reflect upon the last six months traveling through Asia.

In 1998 I took a semester off from college to backpack through China, Nepal, India and Thailand. I arrived in Beijing at a time when China's consumer revolution was only just starting to gain momentum and signs of a modernizing country were everywhere. Skyscrapers were popping up throughout the city and power lines were reaching out to even the most remote villages. Foreigners were only just discovering China's backpacking potential and authorities were scrambling to find ways to accommodate the newcomers. There were even separate tickets for foreigners when taking trains and buses and many parts of the country were still restricted, requiring special permits.

Over the course of two months, I worked my way via bus and train from Beijing to Xi'an along the Silk Road and on to Lanzhou and Dunhuang. From there I went south to Golmud, Lhasa, Mount Kailash, Mount Everest and on to the Nepal border. It was an arduous trip that tested more than just my Chinese language ability. I learned how to bargain. I learned when to trust people and when not to. And most of all, I learned patience. Anyone hoping for Western travel conveniences in China is courting disappointment.

A 36-hour bus ride to Lhasa across the frozen Tibetan Plateau was particularly trying. During bouts of motion sickness and food poisoning, I struggled to keep my composure – along with the contents of my stomach. Watching the sun rise twice, barely moving from a bus seat the entire trip, would be enough to push anyone to the brink of madness. The only pleasant part of the journey was when, midway through the ride, my Irish traveling companion handed an audio cassette up to the bus driver. The driver put it into the stereo and seconds later, traversing Tibet's desolate north in a bus full of Tibetan pilgrims and traders, the speakers boomed the soundtrack of *The Empire Strikes Back*.

I loved the adventure of traveling in China, but there were plenty of occasions when I'd find myself wishing I had some sort of teleportation device to beam myself the hell out of there. Traveling in China brought about new and unexpected challenges. Sometimes I had to walk for hours hauling around my big backpack just to find a hotel that would accept foreigners. I fought my way through mobs of people to get onto buses and trains. I even had to squat in outhouses where nothing but a thin plank of wood separated me from a plunge into neck-deep excrement – a vision that still haunts me.

In Lhasa, Tibet's capital, I met up with nine other foreigners who had posted an announcement on the wall next to the reception desk of my guesthouse looking for another interested traveler to join them for a 10-day 4x4 trip. The tour package included three Land Cruisers, a supply truck and an English-speaking Tibetan guide. The vehicles would take us to Kailash, a holy mountain in southwest Tibet, then on to Everest Base Camp near the Nepal border.

In Tibet, venturing outside of Lhasa needed to be organized through a government tour agency in order to get travel permits. We made the deal with a Tibetan man named Tsedor. Clad in a pinstripe suit and shiny patent leather shoes, Tsedor could have been cast in a Tibetan version of *The Godfather*. He chain-smoked cigarettes as he drew up a contract with us. Smoke flowed up and over his slicked-back black hair as we all signed our names.

From the first day of the trip, the contract that we'd signed with Tsedor was broken at every possible opportunity. Our guide refused to take us to any of the significant places that we had been told we would visit. He then told us that two days would be cut from the end of the trip.

This ultimately resulted in a showdown five days into the trip at three o'clock in the morning in a small monastery on the banks of Lake Manasarovar in western Tibet. Our drivers, along with the guide, snuck out of bed while we were all sleeping and drove off with our travel permits. The alarm was sounded by one of my travel partners who heard the guide making his getaway. In sub-freezing temperatures and still wrapped in my down sleeping bag, I tried to chase down the deserters, but all I got was a face full of dust as the spinning tires tore away down the dirt road.

Even though I was the youngest of our crew, I was put in charge of dealing with our new problem as I was the only one who spoke any Chinese. I hitchhiked with a few of my travel mates for about four hours to an army post where I relayed the story of our abandonment. In Tibet, traveling without permits is strictly prohibited, but the officers that we spoke with took pity on our situation and forced Tsedor to send out replacement jeeps and a new guide. It took three days for them to reach us, so we had time to hike the 52-kilometer pilgrimage around Mount Kailash.

Mount Kailash is considered by close to a billion people in Asia to be among the most sacred mountains in the world. Hindus, Buddhists, Jains and Bons look forward to the day when they might get to make the holy trek around the mountain. Pilgrims from all over follow the worn trail that climbs to elevations over 5,500 meters (18,000 ft.) – higher even than Everest base camp. It takes three days for the typical pilgrim to complete a circumambulation, but it is said that the most experienced can do it in one day.

The most devout pilgrims prostrate with each step around the mountain. They kneel, reach out their arms, lay flat touching their foreheads to the ground, take one more step and repeat the process. For these pilgrims it can take weeks to complete the circuit. Each prostration is meant to cleanse karmic accumulation and gain a position one step closer to enlightenment. It is said by some believers that 108 completed journeys around Kailash is a shortcut to enlightenment, and many devote years to this task, prostrating each step of the way.

Overly confident in my fitness, I decided that I would try to do the hike in one day. I woke at four o'clock in the morning, shouldered my bag and set off on my own into the freezing darkness. With my headlamp as the only light, it was difficult to decipher which path was the correct one. I knew that the mountain had hosted pilgrims for thousands of years so I was surprised that the trail wasn't more worn in. I continued on until the trail dead-ended right at the base of the mountain's south face. Only then did I know for sure that I'd gone the wrong way; but there wasn't much I could do but sit, sip on water and wait for the sun to rise.

I sat there in the dark completely alone. Never in my life had I felt so isolated. The whole point of my trip was to run away and immerse myself in a different culture, one where there were no expectations of me. But as I sat there with nothing but silence and the ghostly white mountain towering behind me, I began to question my motives. Real solitude was not quite as comforting as I had expected.

Kailash too is on its own. It sits by itself a few hundred kilometers north of the Himalayas, not really a part of any range. It is an odd mountain in that it seems to have grown all on its own with four distinct slopes accurately facing the four directions.

The southern face of the mountain took on an eerie blue color as the sun began to rise. I sat watching the first rays of sunlight shoot across the tips of the highest Himalayan peaks far in the distance. They lit up with purple, then dark red, then orange, casting long shadows onto smaller, neighboring peaks. The world's largest mountain range looked rather small from where I sat.

Just as the sun started to show itself over the horizon, I heard footsteps behind me. I watched a small, disheveled man feel his way along a narrow trail with a long cane. He shouted to me, but I did not understand. I used my best Chinese but he didn't seem to understand me either. Instead, he responded with, "Cha! Cha! (Tea! Tea!)" and he waved his arms for me to follow him. He led me to a small stone hut on a nearby slope. When I got closer, I could see that his eyes were mostly closed and appeared to be scabbed over – perhaps the consequence of too much sun exposure. He must have been nearly blind, but he effortlessly poured me a cup of salty yak butter tea. I was chilled to the bone and the tea was smooth and warmed my core. I sipped it with pleasure even though the oily flavor confused my taste buds.

He said nothing more and neither did I. He likely never even knew that I was a foreigner. But he knew that I was alone and that I needed to warm up. I refused a second cup and he smiled with rotted teeth. Then he waved me to follow him and he pointed west at a small path, gesturing for me to follow it over the hill. I thanked him and did as he said. A few hours later, I reunited with my travel companions and we did the trek together in a more reasonable three days.

When we returned from the hike, our new 4x4s and new guide were awaiting us. They were to take us to the Nepal border, but only after a visit to Everest base camp on the Tibet side of the Himalayas. One night, at a small roadside guesthouse, we sipped on hot water trying to fight off altitude sickness and the screaming headaches that accompany it. Life at over 5,000 meters high is not easy. Even just walking a few steps can leave one winded.

At one table on the other side of the room, I saw a young foreign woman sitting among gambling truck drivers. She was beautiful and totally out of place – and she was looking at me. I blushed once we made eye contact, but I was too shy to say anything. My more outgoing travel companion asked her, "How the hell did you end up out here?"

She turned with a stern look that seemed to ask, "Why the hell wouldn't I be out here?" But her glare soon softened. "I snuck in," she said. "I was in Nepal and I didn't want to pay the $100 for the Tibet permit, so I hitched a ride across the border."

Her name was Margarita and she spoke with a sexy Russian accent that instantly sparked my crush on her. We didn't say much to each other that night because my travel companions were a talkative bunch, but every once in a while, I was pretty sure she was giving me flirtatious glances. Later that night, alone in my bed, I ridiculed myself for not taking more initiative. I knew that I'd probably never get to cross paths with Margarita again.

We set off early the next morning and made our way to the Nepal border. There, the guide abruptly confiscated our passports and demanded that we pay an extra fee for the new vehicles and guide. When we refused to pay, the guide suddenly bolted with our passports in hand. I pursued him through the twisting roads of the border town. He wound in and out of small alleyways as if he was trying to lose me, but I stayed with him stride for stride. It felt like a scene from an old Chinese kung fu movie as I chased the villain along ancient stone streets. I was thrilled by the chase but afraid of what awaited me at the end of it.

The pursuit ended at the office of a top immigration official. He was the one responsible for granting permission for foreigners to cross from China to Nepal. He was obviously in on the scam, as he refused to return our passports unless we paid the demanded sum. The deliberations were ugly as at first he did not seem open to compromising. But eventually we managed to negotiate a deal. It would still cost us all a good chunk of cash, but far less than they had originally asked for. I collected our passports and returned to my travel companions, who, to my surprise, were chatting with Margarita. She too had gotten caught up at the border.

I lost my breath, started sweating and tried to compose myself. I'd semi-heroically chased down a man through a dangerous border town and contended with the local mafia, but when it came to talking with Margarita, I was a basket case. "Just don't ask, 'What the hell are you doing here?'" I thought to myself.

That night she invited me to join her at a local disco and I watched her dance, too bashful to join in. But she was patient with me and asked me to meet her for dinner in Kathmandu the following evening.

After dealing with the madness of the Tibet trip, I was ready to leave China for good. My patience had been tested to the point of giving up. As I walked across the Friendship Bridge spanning the Bhote Koshi River that separates China from Nepal, I was preparing to throw my Chinese-English dictionary over the bridge, ceremonially cutting myself off from China for good. But by the time I passed the bridge's midpoint, a hint of sadness, something close to homesickness, came over me. China had twisted me into a different person. I survived more arguments and stressful situations in those two months than I had in my entire life, but those experiences were more than just annoyances, they had made me stronger. I was no longer the timid 21-year-old afraid of confrontation.

If anything, China had made me strangely addicted to confrontation. Moreover, I think I was somehow addicted to China itself.

I looked back across the bridge from Nepal to China, and even as I cursed the place, I knew I'd have to return.

In Kathmandu, while my travel companions began planning treks and raft trips, I prepared for dinner with Margarita. I went to the restaurant she had suggested and anxiously awaited her arrival. But instead of Margarita, in came all seven of my travel companions. They hadn't intended to pick the same restaurant, but since I was sitting alone, they insisted I join them at their table. Margarita came in a few minutes later, saw the crew that I sat with, approached the table and said, "Sorry I can't stay, but I've got other plans."

I knew she didn't have other plans. She thought that I'd invited everyone to *our* dinner and she was disappointed with me. She walked out and I let her go.

Over the next two weeks, I worked my way east by boat, by foot and by bus to Darjeeling and Sikkim in India before ending up in Kolkata. And by seemingly impossible coincidence, there she was again, a lovely smile sneaking across her face.

"*We* were supposed to have dinner," Margarita scolded me.

"I know," I said. "I'm sorry. I didn't plan on them coming."

"Well, too bad I am only seeing you now," her words rolled flirtatiously off of her tongue. "I have a flight to Bangkok tonight."

"Really? I'll be there in three days," I said enthusiastically. "Maybe we can try for dinner again?"

She thought for a minute, debating whether or not to give me another chance. "I'm going to a retreat in Chiang Mai for a week," she said. "Wanna join?"

"Sounds like fun," I said, trying my best not to reveal my mounting enthusiasm. It seemed that maybe I was destined to hook up with Margarita.

Two days later I packed my bags and prepared for my flight the following morning. I went to sleep with nervous thoughts of my next meeting with the Russian beauty. I worried that maybe she wouldn't wait for me or that somehow I'd find a way to screw up again.

At two o'clock in the morning, I awoke with an excruciating headache.

Malaria attacks people in different ways. For me it was a swelling in my brain that pushed hard on the back of my eyeballs, incapacitating me with pain. For four days I suffered from severe fever and nausea. The symptoms finally dissipated on the fifth day and I was released from the hospital. I imagined Margarita's disappointment. I'd failed again, and this time I would not get another chance.

I chose to spend my last week in Asia alone on a small island beach in Thailand, recovering from both my malaria and my total failure with Margarita. I had hoped for a week of rest and relaxation before the conclusion of my Asia adventure. Instead, I found myself face-to-face with a shark.

It was like a cartoon, the typical shark scene where the beast encircles some poor fool before showing its prey row after row of razor-sharp teeth. I was that fool. But I still thought that I just might be able to beat back the shark if it made a move to harm me. It was definitely big, but not much bigger than me. If it attacked, I was ready to defend myself.

My confidence disintegrated the moment a second shark arrived. I could feel my heart race as I imagined my life ending in a bloodbath. I did my best to keep both sharks in view and not let either sneak up from behind me. When the pair completed another half-circle around me, I caught sight of a third shark. A primal scream unlike anything that had ever come from my body erupted through the spout of my snorkel. I panicked and began thrashing to the shore 60 meters away.

I swam faster than I had in my entire life. My form was terrible, and I must have looked like an injured seal. This was not exactly the appearance I wanted, but instinct had taken over, suppressing any rational action. While my arms frantically splashed in and out of the water, the first shark kept pace with tauntingly little exertion. Its left eye stayed level with my right eye just an arm's reach away.

I saw a small rock outcropping up ahead and swam straight for it. I was nearly there when the shark darted and cut right in front of me as if he knew this might be his last chance to literally scare the shit out of me. I reached for the rocks and pulled myself out of the water. Jagged shells and sharp limestone tore up the soles of my feet. My heels had been made soft by hours of swimming in the salty water. I stood quivering on the small rock, blood oozing from my injuries, still 20 meters from shore. The last thing I wanted to do was jump back into the water and leave a trail of blood in my wake, but my options were limited, so after a couple of minutes I dove back in and swam for the beach.

I made it safely to shore, but the cuts on my feet were severe and needed proper bandaging. I still had a two-kilometer hike separating me from the island's only ranger station, so I wrapped myself up with the bits of gauze and tape left over from my medical kit, packed up the tent, and made the trek, limping and trembling with shock the entire way.

I finally reached the island's main port and knocked on the park ranger's office door. He spoke very little English and the only word he seemed to recognize was "shark."

"No shark here," he said confidently.

"Yes," I said. "Three sharks."

"No. No shark here," he said again.

With that argument seemingly settled, I asked for help with my injuries. There were rivulets of blood dripping down the sides of my sandals and my little first aid kit was ill-equipped to treat the wounds.

"Do you have bandages for my feet?" I asked.

"Shark no do that," he said. "No shark here."

"Okay, you're right, no shark!" I shouted. "I cut myself shaving! Now do you have a medical kit?"

I did the best I could to bandage up my feet. There were no boats to the mainland that day, so I had to spend another night in my tent alone, reliving the encounter over and over. Every time I tried to close my eyes to sleep I felt like I was right back in the water, the sharks circling.

I pulled out my Walkman and tried to tune into any radio station available. I needed to hear someone else's voice. I came across a station broadcast from India. It was a dating talk show in English. For a few hours, I tried to distract myself with the issues of dating in modern India. But soon my Walkman's batteries ran out and I was alone again.

In the unnerving silence, I thought back to my travels. I thought back to my almost-blind guide on Mount Kailash, to Tsedor and the Tibetan mafia, and to Margarita and malaria. I thought back to all the beautiful places I'd been and all of the lovely people I'd met. But most of all, I started thinking about when I'd get back to China.

CHAPTER 3

CHINA'S DAMMED

I saw the movie "Never Cry Wolf" when I was six years old at the small independent theater around the corner from my home in Denver. The story followed a biologist named Tyler Smith who was sent to the Canadian arctic to study the recent decline of caribou herds. The arctic wolf was the main suspect in the caribou's disappearance and Tyler's job was to investigate this.

In the story, a biplane drops him off in the middle of the frozen tundra, and after surviving multiple encounters with the dangers of wilderness living, Tyler is rescued by a wandering Inuit elder. The Inuit becomes a mentor to Tyler, and soon Tyler decides to abandon his life back in the city altogether to pursue a new life in the wilderness.

This story became my fantasy. Even at such a young age, I knew that I too would eventually make my life in the wilderness.

In high school, and later in college, I was always planning an escape of some sort. I had convinced myself that a life of true contentment could only be found in the wild. I admired writers like Henry David Thoreau, Jack London and Edward Abbey who idealized lives removed from society. I was fascinated by the survival techniques of Native Americans and studied all of Tom Brown Junior's wilderness survival guides. The outdoors became my sanctuary from the city.

In college I took a three-week solo backpacking trip to the Wind Rivers mountain range in Wyoming. I hiked for days, carrying my little ax and fearing grizzly bears with every step. I encountered only a few people, including one on horseback who scolded me for not carrying a gun to protect myself from bears. On the third day I camped at a high alpine lake near a couple of mountaineers who had spent the day on high alpine crags. I shared a bottle of wine with them that I had lugged up the valley in my backpack. In return, they shared their peace pipe, and together we watched the sun set over the Rocky Mountains.

I returned to college after that trip and became increasingly interested in the study of different Asian histories, cultures and religions. I pursued degrees in both Asian studies and anthropology. During my second year at the University of Colorado I took a class called Asian Perceptions of Nature. The fact that classes like this even existed made me appreciate school. At one point in the semester we spent about a month just studying the writings of Japanese and Chinese hermits.

I found inspiration in the wandering writings of Bashō, Saigyō and Han Shan. They were all hermit poets who had abandoned society to roam about the mountains, living simple lives and writing poetry. Many of their writings only survived because of followers who transcribed what the poets had scribbled on leaves or rocks before discarding them.

Soon I had China on my mind, and if I have to answer honestly why I came to China the first time, I think this would be the answer: "Before I disappeared into the mountains forever, I might at least give the rest of the world a try first."

I saved what I could and borrowed some money from my parents. This provided the means for my first trip to Asia where I met Margarita and the sharks. Back then I had no idea of what to expect. I even left a kind of last will and testament with my housemates just in case something happened and I never returned.

Through those travels in China and Tibet, I never found any of the hermits I sought. However, I did find something else, something different. It wasn't anything I could describe as better, but it was most definitely different. In China's countryside, I found people able to live the way I'd always admired. They grew their own food, raised their own animals, built their own homes and even distilled their own liquor. Dreams of running away to the mountains faded away as all of my attention was on China. And in August 2000, I returned for my second trip.

In order to receive my degree in Asian Studies, I needed to finish my senior thesis – a study of the Three Gorges Dam and the social impact of the dam's relocation effort. An estimated 2 to 3 million people lived within the areas that would be flooded by the massive reservoir formed behind the dam. I was interested in the consequences of moving so many people. My library research was finished, but I still needed to do some field work to complete the paper. After attending my friends' wedding in Bali, Indonesia, I worked my way up the coast of Malaysia and Thailand before flying to Kunming and on to Chongqing.

Chongqing was still a relatively sleepy city on a steep hillside when I first visited. Ten years later, however, the Three Gorges Dam would allow the city to spread out onto what was previously an uninhabitable floodplain. In the years that followed, Chongqing would earn the distinction of being the fastest growing urban center on the planet.

I departed from Chongqing on a boat that would float down the Yangtze River for three days to Yichang, the city closest to the site of the colossal dam. I wasn't interested in the dam itself, but wanted to meet the people who would be losing their homes over the coming years as the reservoir flooded their land.

The big number was 135. All along the valley it was posted on big billboards in bold red print telling the number of meters the water was expected to rise. Sometimes the sign was displayed right on top of people's homes. These were homes that would have to go to make way for the reservoir.

I left the boat after the first night and started hiking along the river. I came upon a small farmhouse where an old lady eyed me suspiciously. A skinny dog leaped out onto the dirt road to greet me with vicious growls and barks. I reached for the nearest loose rock and readied myself to hurl it if the dog attacked, but one angry command from the old lady made the dog curl his tail and scoot away sheepishly.

An older man stepped out of the small house. Apparently curious about what a foreigner was doing on his property, he waved me over to the courtyard. The dog did a quick circle around me, sizing me up as I entered.

The man sat me down on a small stool, poured me a cup of tea and placed a plate full of sunflower seeds in front of me. My Chinese language skills at that time were not great and had only slightly improved since my adventure in Tibet two years earlier. We started up a simple conversation, and the man told me his name was Zhou, pronounced like "Joe."

"How long has your family lived on this land?" I asked.

"A long time," he said as the slender dog lay down at his feet. "Longer than I can remember."

"Will you have to move soon?" I asked, already knowing the answer.

"See those buildings up there?" he said, pointing to a distant cluster of bleach-white buildings far up on the hillside. "Next year, we are supposed to move there with our two daughters. But we can't just leave our land behind, so we'll stay here until the water covers everything."

The relocated were typically given apartments in new urban areas constructed by the government high up on the rim of the valley. They were also given cash for compensation. The amount would be considered substantial by any small farmer, but without the farm to provide a sustainable income and steady source of food, many would soon learn that city life is far more expensive.

As I continued my hike, I noticed other new urban centers along the valley rim. They looked out of place among the green terraced hillsides. For those who already lived in the older urban centers that would be flooded, the move would be relatively easy. Basically, their towns were just relocated, with similar housing, and the inhabitants would continue to live a lifestyle similar to what they were used to. But for families like the Zhous, the move involved more than just packing and unpacking. It meant a drastic shift in lifestyle. They would no longer have their farms of rice and vegetables. They would no longer be able to raise their pigs and chickens. These were not families who were accustomed to buying vegetables and meat at the market. And they were definitely not used to sitting in sixth-floor apartments with only televisions to keep them company.

My investigation went on for several days. Everyone else I met along the valley seemed wary of my motives and appeared to be uncomfortable telling me anything about the relocation. I rarely received the candor that Mr. Zhou provided.

At one point, a police car met me at a crossroads and the officers inside asked me to join them in the car. A number of opponents of the Three Gorges Dam construction, some of them well-known activists, had been imprisoned for their protests. As I got into the police car, I worried that maybe I too had crossed the line between observer and troublemaker.

It turned out that they just wanted me to register at the local police station, standard practice for law enforcement. The officer in charge was very hospitable and he seemed genuinely interested in what would compel a lone foreigner to visit his small town. I told him about my thesis and he offered to be my personal guide for my remaining two days in the area.

He drove me up to one of the empty cities that lined the ridges above the valley. The roads were freshly laid, the storefronts were brand-new and everything was clean and tidy. It was unsettling to realize that there wasn't a single person living in the entire city. It was like a ghost town but too new to even have ghosts. Most of the farmers who would have to leave their villages due to the coming reservoir would be moved to cities like this one.

I soon understood that the plan was not just forced relocation, it was forced urbanization. This was the new China, one where cities would continue to grow as villages disappeared. In the case of the Three Gorges relocation, urbanization was mandated as part of the dam project. The rest of China would face a similar fate on a much larger scale, but instead of villagers urbanizing to avoid the flood, they would move to join the flood of migrant workers spilling into the cities. This migration would be the engine that would drive China's growth.

China was changing fast and everything that I had learned about China in college would be ancient history by the time the migration was finished. So if I was ever going to understand modern China, I would have to be there to watch it all happen.

CHAPTER 4

MOVING EAST

Highway 26 through Mount Hood National Forest in central Oregon was covered with a fresh sprinkling of rain. We were cruising by campgrounds and sequoia forests when the tires suddenly lost traction. I'd just removed my seat belt to get the *Smith Rock Climbing Guide* from the back seat, while Zan steered the Toyota 4-Runner. The truck struggled to maintain friction and the rear wheels skidded.

Zan tried to correct the vehicle, but we skidded even farther in the other direction. An alarm sounded inside me and sent adrenaline rushing to my brain. I put my left arm across Zan's waist and muttered, "It's okay." It came out calmly, like I'd been in the situation before and it was no big deal, as if we were at the precipice of a harmless roller coaster ride and there was no need to panic.

The vehicle hurtled sideways down the wet highway, then the wheels caught a dry patch and the car abruptly flipped hard onto the roof. The impact sent my head through the sunroof, smashing into the asphalt of the road. It was hard and fast, and I didn't even have time to catch a breath before we were somehow back upright with the car again on its wheels facing forward.

I looked at Zan and she looked at me. We were both pleading for some grasp on reality. But our senses had yet to catch up. We had flipped an SUV at high speed, rotated a full 360 degrees, then landed back on the tires facing forward. Considering the magnitude of the accident, it was far too orderly an outcome to be real. But the jagged windshield angled toward our throats let us know just how lucky we were to have survived.

"Are you okay?" I asked.

"Yeah, I guess so," she said. "You?"

The fresh scents from the surrounding pine forest suddenly dissolved into an oddly familiar aroma, something I knew I'd smelled before, but couldn't remember when. As the words "I think I'm fine" started to roll off my tongue, I noticed a salty metallic flavor in my mouth. I went to wipe off what I thought was sweat from my brow and realized that blood was erupting from the top of my head. It flowed down my face. Zan scrambled to find something for me to cover it with, ultimately handing me a nearly finished paper towel roll.

A witness to the accident pulled to the side of the road and opened Zan's door to help her out. The woman comforted her for a few minutes while I waited for someone to come help me. No one did, so I steadied myself and got out to join Zan. I walked around to the other side of the car to see her huddled by a gathering of other people who had stopped to help. "Don't mind me, I'm fine," I told the crowd.

Blood stained so much of my clothing that I guess no one really wanted to get too close, though one stranger eventually handed me a clean towel that I used to apply pressure to my head. Zan and I encouraged each other to take some slow breaths and stay calm as we waited for the EMTs to arrive.

By the time they came, we were as calm and collected as could be expected. We were hydrated, discussing what to do next and feeling really lucky to be alive as we looked over the truck. But that calm quickly gave way to panic when the EMTs came sprinting toward us out of the ambulance, as if we were on fire and they had only seconds to put us out. They were clearly concerned and started asking all sorts of rapid-fire medical questions.

"Wait, wait. Slow down," I pleaded. Their unnerving arrival at the accident was taking its toll on me. The blood loss and shock had combined to slow the flow of oxygen to my brain. What started as a dark spot in the right side of my vision grew and grew until all was black and I went unconscious.

I awoke about 30 minutes later immobilized on a backboard and in a helicopter with two angelic women hovering over me. "Ah, you're awake," one of them said. "We're going to go ahead and take your pants off for you if that's okay?

"Uh, okay," I stuttered. I wasn't really sure where I was and what had happened, but I wasn't in a position to protest.

"Don't worry, we'll take it easy on you," the other woman said, smiling. "If we don't remove your pants now, once you get into the emergency room they are going to cut them off."

As soon as the helicopter landed on the roof of Seattle's Swedish Medical Center, the pretty faces of the helicopter nurses shifted into the distance. I didn't even have time to thank them for saving my pants before I was lost among a horde of doctors surrounding me.

"My name is Suzy and I'm going to take your blood pressure," said one, as the rest of the doctors hurriedly rolled my gurney from the rooftop toward the emergency room.

"My name is Jonathan and I'm going to take a blood sample," said another.

"My name is Angela," said another. "Can you open your mouth and say 'Ahh'?" It was mechanical and rehearsed and all relatively painless until Ralph showed up.

"My name is Ralph and I'm going to stick my finger up your rectum." I convinced myself that he must have been looking for internal bleeding; but to this day I still don't know for sure whether Ralph was a doctor or just another patient who happened by my stretcher and wanted in on the fun.

After some ugly stitches, I was released from the hospital and spent the next few weeks recovering with a little bald patch on my head where they had shaved off my hair. Zan's insurance company called to cut me a check for $1,000 for my pain and suffering from my accident. I eagerly accepted the money, not realizing that I'd herniated a disc in my neck.

Though the $1,000 could fund my next trip to China, it would never be sufficient compensation for the neck pain and sleeping problems that would plague me for the next 15 years.

During my recovery back in Boulder, Colorado, I returned to work as a waiter in a small jazz bar. My coworker Brett told me that his brother was visiting from China and that I should ask him for some acupuncture treatments to deal with some of the pain and stiffness I had after the accident. That's how I met Josh Pollock.

Josh seemed to take sadistic pleasure in torturing me with needles. When treating me, he resembled a mad scientist, laughing maniacally with every painful twist of the needles. He was a licensed Traditional Chinese Medicine (TCM) doctor, and he was actually quite talented, but at times I wondered if the point of TCM was to cause enough pain in certain spots so that one forgot about whatever ailment was actually causing the initial discomfort.

Josh gave me the treatments in exchange for shots of top-shelf whiskey at the bar. He told me about his life in China and the martial arts temple above the small town of Dali where he and his brother had studied. I had been to China twice, but always as a visitor, a tourist. Never had I considered actually living there.

I'd spent five years at CU Boulder becoming an aficionado of Asian histories, philosophies, geographies and arts. My anthropology studies made it so that on command I could go into great detail about the physical and cultural evolution of our species. I regretted none of what I had learned, but Asian studies and Anthropology degrees were not exactly valuable commodities in the job market.

For the foreseeable future, I was on a trajectory to be a waiter. It was a job that I actually really liked, but it wasn't going to open any doors to bigger and better things. The more I thought about the kung fu mountain temple where the Pollock brothers had lived, the more my curiosity stewed. It wasn't exactly the hermitage I'd sought on my first trip to China, but it might be the closest I'd ever get.

The accident was the last push I needed to leave, and late in 2001, I quit my job, cashed in the insurance check and packed up to move to China.

CHAPTER 5

A NEW HOME

I spent nearly three months training five hours a day, six days a week, in the mountains near Dali at the Wuwei Temple. Wuwei, meaning "natural action" or "actionless action," is a Shaolin-style temple surrounded by dense pine forests and Buddhist statues. At the time, it was one of the few martial arts temples in China that accepted foreigners. The training was vigorous. Every day ended with satisfied grunts as I lay my aching body down to sleep.

The monks were up at four o'clock every morning to chant sutras, but the foreign students were allowed to sleep until seven. We were then supposed to go for a run, stretch, eat a breakfast of vegetarian noodles or stuffed buns, train for three hours, eat lunch, rest for a few hours, train for two more hours, eat dinner and usually fall asleep exhausted by nine o'clock. The temple housed between two and 10 foreign students and about eight monks, some of them orphaned children taken in by the temple.

After my first three days at the temple, my body felt like a badly beaten piñata. The training used muscles, tendons and ligaments I'd never used before, and every one of them was screaming in agony. Stretching was an important part of the training to gain flexibility and prevent injury. Line drills with kicking and punching worked even more on flexibility and also built up muscle mass and speed. There were the other exercises meant to toughen skin and bone, either by boxing the sand-filled punching bag or by repeatedly thrusting your hands into a large ceramic container filled with dried corn kernels.

By week three I could nearly do the splits and was pulling off aerial kick-flips. Considering my flailing inabilities on the day of my arrival, this to me was an impressive feat. I was also attempting to teach myself acupuncture – not my best idea, but each night before bed I'd send long needles deep into my flesh where my acupuncture map indicated the most important points were.

The temple was nestled up in the mountains just above the small town of Dali in western Yunnan Province. The temple had no electricity, served only vegetarian food, had strict policies regarding training commitments and had very eccentric head master. "Shifu," as we called him, was a short balding man with a long gray goatee and the countenance of an ancient sage. He always wore a yellow and orange robe that distinguished him as the temple master, and he demanded the respect that came with the title. His presence at training assured a diligent session with the monks scrambling to do everything perfectly to avoid reprimand.

Most foreign students didn't stay more than a week or two. My longer commitment, much like Josh and Brett before me, earned Shifu's trust and friendship. Shifu showed his affection in only one way – astoundingly painful pinches on the arm that left the ugliest dark blue bruises. Every time Shifu yelled at me, saying my stance was off balance or my kicks were not high enough, he'd emphasize the scolding by what felt like ripping a hole in my arm. The new students looked at me with strange envy, wishing that they could earn the same painful marks of accomplishment.

We practiced ancient martial arts forms that often felt more like dance moves than combat. But the better I got at them, the more interesting they became. Some forms required weapons like swords, sabers and staffs, but I focused on the Eagle Claw, an aggressive form based on grabs and locks. What we studied was rudimentary at best, but the exercise was intense, and I was soon fitter than I'd ever been.

I was planning to extend my stay another three months when, on one especially chilly morning, I was practicing handless kip-ups on the cold stone floor. A handless kip-up is a move that instantly springs the practitioner from lying on his back on the ground to standing upright, using nothing but a kick of the legs and a spring of the neck. Midway through a set of 50 repetitions, my neck seized and my head became stuck at a skewed angle. Shifu, the only man at the temple somewhat qualified to tend injuries, had gone off to Kunming to visit his master. This left me with one of the head monks who felt certain that he could twist my head back into place.

"One... two... three," he said as he slowly rocked my head back and forth before violently spinning it halfway around. I yelled out in agony and his expression immediately went from one of total confidence to something more resembling curiosity. Perhaps this treatment was something that he'd seen work on TV and he couldn't understand why it didn't work for me. He resolved that he hadn't done it hard enough, so I hesitantly let him once again take hold of my head. This time he nearly twisted it right off.

Unfortunately, these 'treatments' did more damage to my neck than the injury itself. Not only did this mean the end of my stay at Wuwei Temple, but it turned into an injury that put a serious strain on my ability to do anything. When I was finally able to see a real doctor – one that didn't try to twist my head straight – I learned that I'd herniated a disc in my neck from the car accident a year earlier and had made it worse with my injury at the temple. It was a setback that made me rethink my plans in China. I'd come to Dali to study martial arts; but with that now impossible, I really had no idea what to do.

*　　*　　*

The first day I met Kris Ariel, he knocked me square on the chin with a right hook that sent me spinning to the grass.

It was my first day in Dali when I met Kris at the Sunshine Café. Somehow he convinced me to put on some boxing gloves and go for a round. First I took a few overconfident swings and watched as Kris ducked, dodged. Then he came right at me with a solid strike. Through the stunned green haze, I knew Kris and I would be good friends. To this day, he won't let me forget that defeat.

Kris was born in Hayward, California, raised in Kailua, Hawaii, and after a series of moves ended up in Lawrence, Kansas. A friend of his from Lawrence lived in Dali the previous year, and upon hearing the stories of life in China, Kris made up his mind to go. He knew nothing about China and he didn't know a word of the language, but he had four months of free time before starring in local productions of both *Stewart Little* and *Sacagawea* with a local theater company. On September 16th, 2001, Kris boarded a plane and headed for the East. He has never looked back.

Kris first arrived by bus from Hong Kong to Guangzhou. He had no map, no guide and couldn't find anyone who spoke any English. He wandered around the city for hours unable to find accommodation that accepted foreigners, until a nice old lady led him to a hotel near the train station. Two days later, after a 22-hour train ride and a nine-hour bus ride, Kris arrived in Dali.

Kris hadn't been in Dali for more than a couple of weeks when he started helping out at one of the local tourist cafés. The Sunshine Café was a popular western food restaurant on Dali's locally famous *Yangren Jie* ("Foreigners' Street"), and the owner soon asked Kris to become the café's manager. What was meant to be just a vacation turned into a permanent relocation. He took to living and working in Dali so well that after just a couple of weeks he sent an email back to his theater company telling them to find someone else to play his roles.

The four young girls who worked at the Sunshine Café took time aside every day to teach Kris Chinese and how to cook some local dishes. Kris learned Chinese faster than anyone I've ever met. Whereas most people need at least three years to become proficient in the language, he was basically fluent after one, and he never took a class. In exchange for the girls teaching him, he helped them to improve the Western cuisine that made the Sunshine Café popular among foreign and Chinese tourists alike.

Kris was half Ecuadorean, and from this he had inherited an angled nose, dark hair and tanned skin. Because of his appearance, passing Chinese tourists sometimes confused him as Chinese – an occurrence that Kris would play on by pretending he was from central Asia, rambling in a language that sounded like a sales pitch at a Kyrgyz street market.

Kris became known in Dali for his entertaining antics at the café. Whether he was juggling, walking on stilts or spitting fire, tourists from all over would stop at the café to take photos of his performances. He quickly earned a reputation as one of Dali's surprise attractions.

Dali was an easy place to get stuck. A number of times I'd meet people in town who claimed to just be visiting for a few days, only to bump into them on the streets months, even years, later. A rare self-indulgent sanctuary for China, Dali was a place where foreign backpackers could enjoy putting back a few drinks and munching on wood-fired pizza while exchanging harrowing stories of their travels through China. Because of its historical relevance, it also ranked high on the list of top destinations for Chinese tourists.

Twelve centuries ago, Dali was the seat of Yunnan's Nanzhao Kingdom. At that time, Dali flourished as an international trading hub along the southwestern branches of the Silk Road, connecting eastern China with Southeast Asia and India. Nestled between the Cang Mountains to the west and Erhai, a 40-kilometer-long lake to the east, Dali's natural defenses served well to protect the kingdom. The Bai ethnic group, who established the kingdom, ruled lands throughout Yunnan that stretched west into Tibet and Burma, north into Sichuan, east into Guizhou and south into Laos and Thailand.

The unique and varied geography of Yunnan Province was shaped 50 million years ago during the Eocene Epoch, when India nudged its way into a marriage with the Asian continent, offering up the Himalayas as dowry. Where once the lands were seaside, India's migration assured that Yunnan's future would be far from the sea. As what are known now as Kashmir, Nepal, Bhutan and Tibet rose higher and higher from the violent collision, Yunnan was torn, ripped and stretched like fabric caught up in a sewing machine. The invading subcontinent crashed head-on into Asia, shearing against Yunnan and rippling it with valleys running north to south. The scars left the paths for three of Asia's most important rivers – the Salween, Mekong and Yangtze.

Along with Yunnan's rivers, the birth of the Himalayas was also responsible for creating a geographic diversity unlike anywhere else on the planet. Meili Snow Mountain in Yunnan's northwest reaches an impressive elevation of 6,740 meters. In the east, lush green valleys are filled with limestone karst formations that jut out of the ground like giant cow udders. In the tropical south along the Vietnamese border, where tea, rubber and banana plantations dominate the landscape, the topography plunges to as low as 76 meters above sea level.

The cultural characteristics of the province are at least as diverse. There are 26 recognized ethnic minorities in Yunnan – and even more languages. Han Chinese often find themselves in parts of Yunnan where, even for them, communication is difficult as few speak Mandarin, China's national language. Dali has long been ethnically Bai with a language closer to Burmese and Tibetan than Chinese.

When I first got to Dali it was already a tourist hub. Many like me found themselves content to stay and canceled plans to travel elsewhere. Dali has the kind of charm that makes you want to spend each day at a different café and write the novel you never had the time to work on. It's also a good place to settle down, buy a dog, grow some dreadlocks and spend each day stoned strumming the guitar.

Dali was one of those rare places in China where some history had survived the march of modernization. The town bustled with small businesses run out of old terracotta-roofed homes built of large stone blocks quarried from the nearby mountains. Many villagers in the surrounding countryside lived simple and relatively subsistent lives on their farms. It made for an interesting mix of local farmers, tourists from both China and abroad, and those who had moved to Dali in order to start a business, raise a family or just make Dali their home.

The longer I stayed in Dali, and the more I explored, I too became enamored with the place. Before my injury at the temple, I would meet Kris down in Dali on my day off for brownies and beer at the Sunshine Café. Then we'd usually try to work in a boxing rematch atop Dali's ancient stone wall before whiskeys at the Bird Bar. After my injury, when boxing was no longer possible, there was only the Bird Bar.

Rongjie and Xinmin, a couple from Shandong, left the Beijing art scene to open the Bird Bar in Dali in 2000. Since meeting Rongjie in 2002, I've seen her with long hair, short hair, straight hair, curly hair, dread-locked hair and even rainbow-colored hair. She was known for setting her own style.

Rongjie was also a woman with an exceptional nose. Chinese often talk about foreigners as having a "tall" nose, quite different from the typically smaller Asian nose. Rongjie's was much more pronounced, and it acted as a beacon for her fiery personality. She had the most boisterous laugh and a witty smile that could light up a room.

The Bird Bar resided in a century-old, wood-framed building walled with massive, hand-carved stone blocks. There was a large stone courtyard in the back lined with jasmine and fig trees around a goldfish pond. The bar became Dali's hangout for underground music and art, and for more than a decade it was the heart of Dali's bohemian scene. Customers included film writers and directors, famous Shanghai actors and actresses, tattooed Beijing punk rockers, troubled Chinese youths whose parents sent them to Dali to escape the influences of gang and mafia violence and an assortment of foreigners from all over the world.

For both Kris and me, the Bird Bar became our new home, and I think we both knew that we would not be returning to our old homes. Dali was the future. And one night, perhaps over a few too many whiskeys at the Bird Bar, we had some ideas about how that future might just pan out in our favor.

CHAPTER 6

DOWN TO BUSINESS

I passed the flashlight up to Kris, who shined it so Rongjie could see the ladder rungs. The landlord couldn't find the key to the front door, so we had to scramble in through a broken window in the back. The building was dark and dank, but we managed to climb up a series of ladders and rafters that seemed right out of a game of Donkey Kong.

We entered a small room with an old movie projector that had once illuminated a large theater. At a glance, Kris and I knew that this was where we could build our rock climbing wall and boxing gym. The ceiling was so high that there was enough space to put up full-length climbing routes with a synthetic rock wall.

A small corridor connected the theater to an adjoining room, a room once used as a disco. It had inlaid panel flooring and was ringed with a second floor balcony. With some hard work, we hoped to turn the room into a café and restaurant.

It was nearing winter, and the skies in Dali were clearing up after a long rainy season. November was usually the first month after June that sunny days came to stay – a time of year when chilly breezes rustled leaves turning gold and red, when everyone in Dali was most grateful to be there.

It had been about a month since I'd re-injured my neck at the temple and I was slowly recovering. When we heard that the old movie theater and disco were up for rent, we decided to go for it.

We had no idea what we were getting ourselves into.

The space was in a terrible state. It had all the style and character that one would expect to find in an abandoned warehouse. We would need all new wiring and new flooring to replace the rotten and warped floorboards. The gaping holes in the tarred roofing also required repair.

Perhaps it was overconfidence, or perhaps we were just ignorant, but we thought, "Hey, this is China. It can't cost all that much to fix the place up."

With a friend in the rock climbing business, I got a donation of 60 pairs of used climbing shoes. Other connections could get me discounted ropes and climbing hardware. We figured that this would take care of some of our biggest costs and calculated that we'd need another $10,000 to realize our vision.

I moved back to Colorado that year, to Steamboat Springs, to work during the ski season and raise money for the renovation. For six months, I poured concrete foundations during the day and waited tables in an Italian restaurant at night. I slept in a hammock out back of my friend's condo where he let me stay for free and got out to ski when deep powder snow beckoned. By the next summer, I was ready to return to China with a pocketful of cash to start up our business.

Then I got a devastating email from Kris.

Three days before he was supposed to sign the contract with the landlords of the disco/cinema complex that would commit us to a three-year lease, he got a call telling him that the landlords had backed out of the deal and would no longer rent it to us.

Upon hearing this news, my insides felt empty, like the wind had been knocked right out of me. We thought that we were only months away from starting up our own business, but without the contract, we had nothing.

Little did we know, the setback of losing the contract actually saved us from a much greater misfortune. Only a couple of months later we would be standing next to a large pile of rubble where once the old movie theater and disco had stood.

Even if we'd signed a secure contract that day, we would soon have realized that there was no market for our business in Dali. Kris and I would certainly be good customers, but that would hardly justify the expenses. Dali did get its share of athletic and adventurous tourists, but there could never be enough to cover our overhead. In the end, however, this was a moot point, as the place was scheduled for demolition later that year.

In the wake of China's fast-paced urbanization, property owners frequently lose out. Whether due to large property developments, transportation projects, electricity distribution or just general gentrification, property developers often push people aside for progress, forcing them to relocate. It is a far too common occurrence in China to pay a year's rent up front, and then later find out that developers already had their own ideas.

We learned two fundamental lessons from this experience. First, don't sign a contract without consulting government development plans. Second, remodeling a space always costs much more than expected – especially when enthusiasm and ignorance blind you from realizing that a business idea can quickly turn into a money pit.

We wouldn't have made it through half of the planned renovation before running out of money. Then after already investing so much into it we would have done anything not to back out. We would have borrowed money, taken out a loan, or maxed out a fistful of credit cards to make certain we saw our dream to fruition.

The land-owners Kris and I were dealing with had known the building was going to be knocked down even before our first meeting with them. They were just looking to make a little extra cash from the one-year rental payment that we had agreed to pay up front. If we had paid it, we would have been evicted three months later with no way of reclaiming any of our investment. Luckily for us, our prospective landlords seem to have developed a conscience in the last few days before the contract signing – or maybe they just got nervous about screwing over a couple of foreigners.

I suppose this sort of thing is a rite of passage for many first-time business owners. Making business materialize rarely happens as initially conceived, and it takes more than just ambition and enthusiasm to succeed. At least in our case we were lucky enough still to have our investment money.

Now we just had to figure out what to do with it.

*   *   *

A few weeks after I returned to China, Kris called to tell me about a local restaurant near the Bird Bar that was going out of business. They were asking for roughly $500 to hand over their three-year rental contract on a quaint 120-year-old wooden storefront. The space was too small to do anything like the business we had originally planned, but it was perfect for a simple coffee house and restaurant. The start-up costs would be far more realistic compared to our budget for the gym and café.

Though Dali had a number of choices for Western food, there was nothing in the way of gourmet coffee or quality baked goods. So within three days of learning of the opportunity, Kris and I jumped at it. Soon we had a signed contract and sledge hammers in hand.

The contract gave us a lease for three years at about $200 per month. We tried our best to extend the contract to five years, but the old couple who were our landlords turned down our requests. At a time when property values were already skyrocketing, we couldn't really blame them. They seemed to like us and they earned our trust. They even asked that their daughter become our first employee. This was a request we politely declined. I could only imagine what mishaps might follow if we had to for some reason fire the daughter of our landlord.

Foreigners were not allowed to do business in China on tourist visas, so we had to ask the help of a local friend to sign the contract. His name would have to appear on every license and every contract. Kris and I had seen a number of Chinese and foreign partnerships end disastrously, usually with the foreigner losing out because the Chinese partner held all of the licenses. But with Jinghai, a popular business owner in Dali, we had someone we trusted. Not only was he a close friend, but he was also a respected member of the local community.

The coffee house-to-be was on the bottom floor of a rustic wooden house built in local Bai style, with interlocking wooden beams and walls of stone and mortar. The traditional timber frames were built without any nails or screws, resulting in a structure that would last as long as the wood could hold off the termites.

The previous restaurant owner had done a terrible job creating an appetizing ambience. We tore everything out and spent the next two months at lumber yards, stone mills, paint shops and light stores. We also hired a local family who specialized in woodworking to help us restore the property. They stripped off the white paint that covered up the beautiful solid wood beams and intricate lintels, built a charming wooden entryway to replace the heavy metal doors, constructed a small stage in the corner and completely renovated the kitchen.

From the beginning, Kris and I argued about everything from paint colors to track lighting. We each visualized the coffee house a bit differently and we were both extremely stubborn, but the end result was something that we were both very proud of. Kris's fondness for the abstract and modern and my fondness for natural and classical styles blended in a very comfortable and intimate atmosphere.

We finished construction one month later, in October 2003, and we were the happy owners of a brand new coffee house. Kris was a big fan of Salvador Dali's art, and because we lived in Dali, Kris came up with the name Salvador's Coffee House. After hearing the name for the first time, nothing else sounded right. Salvador's was perfect.

We made a quick trip to Guangzhou to source everything from cheddar cheese and beer to silverware and waffle irons. Guangzhou was also where we found the centerpiece of our restaurant: a Nuova Simonelli Premier Maxi dual-head espresso machine. The machine would set us apart from the other cafés in Dali who all brewed coffee in small stovetop percolators. At Salvador's we would offer espressos, cappuccinos, lattes and mochas using fresh roasts of locally-grown coffee beans.

With a functioning kitchen, a stocked bar and some successful trials making all-natural ice cream, all that was left was to hang a sign in the window with the characters, 招工 ("Help Wanted").

*　*　*

Both Kris and I spent the first month as cooks, bakers, waiters, bartenders, bussers and dishwashers. Business was relatively slow and we managed on our own, but it was unsustainable. We needed help.

A couple who had recently given birth to their first child had hired Mengjuan, a teenage woman from Yunnan's countryside, to help around their house. Once the mother had recovered from birth and the parents were able to handle chores themselves, Mengjuan was no longer needed and was looking for new work. Kris hired her while I was out of town and called me midway through the first day.

"She reorganized the entire kitchen!" he said excitedly. "And she's already making omelets and learning to use the coffee machine!"

This was fantastic news. We had hired two girls before Mengjuan who were so shy that when we spoke to them directly they froze up like deer in headlights. They lasted only a few days before disappearing one night, never to return.

Before Mengjuan, we were worried that Kris and I would soon be overburdened with the responsibilities of maintaining restaurant operations, but Mengjuan proved to be far more capable than both of the other girls put together. Moreover, she was eager to learn, very orderly, a natural with customers and was always smiling. Nothing is more effective in the service industry than a nice smile, and Mengjuan's was radiant.

Mengjuan came from Bangdong Village in Lincang Prefecture near the southwest corner of Yunnan. Bangdong sits high on a valley along the Lancang River, as the upper reaches of the Mekong River are known in China. It is a very fertile part of the province where the majority of farmers live off of the profits of growing and selling tea. The Lincang valleys are lined with man-made terraces laced with tea plants, corn fields, citrus trees, wild raspberries and rice paddies.

In Bangdong, villagers lead cattle and herds of goats along a worn dirt road that snakes down from the main road above. The village is on a steep slope, so that everyone either lives above or below each other. For this reason, Mengjuan never learned how to ride a bicycle.

Bangdong was without electricity until Mengjuan was in first grade, when power began to come on for one or two hours each night. When she was in fourth grade, one family in the village got a television. They charged a small fee for others to come over and watch.

As a child, Mengjuan helped her parents in the tea fields, but when there was free time she played in the hills with the neighborhood children. Life, however, was often difficult.

"Sometimes there wasn't enough to eat," she told me. "I had to help my parents forage for wild mushrooms in the forest just to get food on our plates."

Her father died while she was in middle school and when her mother remarried, her new stepfather insisted she help on the farm instead of attending school. Traditionally, young women in the countryside are supposed to obey their parents' wishes, but Mengjuan was more rebellious, and at age 15 she left home and moved to Dali to find work and start a new life on her own.

When Mengjuan came to Dali she had no experience in the service industry and had never worked in a restaurant, but she took to working at Salvador's with natural grace. It was soon apparent that Kris and I would not have to shoulder the burdens of the restaurant on our own. We taught Mengjuan how to mix ice cream, flip omelets, boil bagels and make foamy cappuccinos. The more we taught her, the less we had to do on our own.

Over the next few years, many more girls from the countryside would join us at Salvador's Coffee House. They would become far more important to Kris and me than we ever could have expected.

CHAPTER 7

A New Partnership

In 1992, Josh Pollock watched his brother Brett fall 20 meters over a waterfall in Costa Rica. Brett had nearly stepped on a coiled pit viper, one of the world's most poisonous and aggressive snakes. When he reached for a tree limb to pull himself out of the reach of the snake's strike, the branch snapped, sending Brett careening down the cliff side. He landed hard on his back on the rocks below.

Josh scrambled down the trail, his long blond dreadlocks flopping about, expecting to find his brother dead. When he rounded the corner, he was surprised to see his brother not only alive, but sitting upright. His forearm, however, was bent where it shouldn't be. He'd broken his arm and the bone had torn right through his flesh below the elbow. He'd also badly hurt his back and had a large cut down the back of his leg. Josh was afraid to leave his brother's side, so together they stumbled and limped for four hours to get out of the jungle.

They made it to a small town where they borrowed money from the local villagers to fly him to the nearest hospital. But the doctors there said they were ill-equipped and there was nothing they could do. After three days of excruciating pain, they finally made it to a hospital in San Jose where it took the strength of three doctors to pull his bone back into place.

For Josh, the experience was traumatizing and he vowed to never let an injury or illness make him feel so powerless again. Two years later, Josh enrolled at the Ruseto Center of Oriental Medicine in Boulder,

Colorado, where he became a certified doctor of Traditional Chinese Medicine. In 1998 he joined his brother Brett in Chengdu, China, to continue his education. There they took an apartment one floor below a young Japanese woman named Naoko Okano.

Josh and Naoko fell in love one Halloween night in Chengdu. She wore a gray gardener's suit, work boots, and a construction worker's hat. Slung over her shoulder was a large fertilizer spray-bottle filled with beer. Josh wore a full-body hazmat suit and didn't leave Naoko's side all night long. One friend says, "I remember Josh's shoes outside Naoko's room for a couple days while she went M.I.A."

I met Naoko on my return to China after meeting Josh in Boulder. I'd come to Kunming with all of my belongings and Josh and Naoko were kind enough to put me up in their apartment before moving to Dali. Naoko was studying Chinese medicine at the time, and once when I asked her opinion about an upset stomach that had been bothering me for a few days she told me, "You need more flesh flute."

I couldn't remember anything like that from the Chinese medicine books and I wasn't sure I wanted it, even if it would help cure my digestive problem.

"*Flesh flute*, you know, like apples and bananas," she said.

"Ah, *fresh fruit*," I said, relieved. "That I can do."

Naoko, like many Japanese, often had troubles with Ls and Rs when speaking English. This sometimes resulted in amusing malapropisms, such as when *long road* came out *wrong load*, *late flight* came out *rate fright* or *razor blades* came out *laser braids*.

Naoko was born and raised in Tamano, a small Japanese town surrounded by rice fields, pear tree groves and wild azalea flowers. As a girl, she tended the family's rice paddies with her mother and grandparents. Later, when her father's plumbing business picked up, she helped with the accounting. But she loved the wilderness, and often got out of work to walk along the nearby beach or hike through Tamano's evergreen forests.

In March 1997, Naoko graduated from Shujitsu University in Okayama with a degree in world history, specializing in China's Silk Road. During her studies she was part of an archaeology study group that traveled to Chengdu in Central China. The trip opened up a whole new world to her and she was hooked on China, determined to return.

After graduation, Naoko worked at a travel agency for half a year with the sole purpose of saving enough money to get back to China. One year later, equipped with a fertilizer spray canister full of beer, she met her future husband.

Josh and Naoko lived one more year in Chengdu before traveling together to Dali. There they studied martial arts at Wu Wei Temple for six months before moving to Kunming, where she became the first foreigner to graduate from Yunnan Traditional Chinese Medicine School.

When Kris and I started Salvador's in Dali, we looked forward to visits from Josh and Naoko. They were very helpful in the initial phases of our business, and they were also two of Salvador's biggest fans – especially when it came to chocolate-chip cranberry banana bread. So when Josh and Naoko asked us to host their wedding reception, we were more than happy to oblige.

On January 21, 2004, Josh's brother Brett led a beautiful ceremony under the falling blossoms of a peach tree at a nearby park. Later, friends and family of Josh and Naoko all met up at Salvador's. With Kris on drums, me on guitar and Brett on lead guitar and vocals, we jammed out some old blues tunes and managed to feed a few dozen people.

The wedding was a kind of validation for Salvador's. Our idea was no longer just some hobby or pipe dream. We were a legitimate business, and Salvador's had made its name in Dali. The café culture was still in its early stages in China so our homemade ice cream, fancy espresso drinks and Western-style baked goods made for a business model that was not only unique to Dali, but also to many of China's major cities. On a daily basis we had visitors asking, "Why don't you guys open a place in Kunming?"

It was a fair question, but one that was easily answered. "Well, we don't live in Kunming."

Kunming was a big city far from everything that I loved about Dali. I loved how close Dali was to the mountains. I loved how life in Dali flowed at the pace of a small rural village. I loved the clean air and water. I loved picking wild raspberries up in the forest. And I loved finishing off every day with a few whiskeys at the Bird Bar. Kunming had none of that. In my mind, Kunming was just another big, dirty city, far from the 'good life' found in Dali. But there was one thing that Kunming did have that Dali lacked – loads of potential customers.

With close to 4 million people, Kunming was a very different market from Dali. In Dali, customers arrived in droves during peak tourist seasons, but we often stayed empty during the off seasons. Business was tied to seasonal tourist fluctuations. Kunming, however, had a local population that could sustain a more steady business model. Since the late 1990s, many families had made small fortunes in property, tea, tobacco and mining, and as the cost of living in Shanghai and Beijing continued to rise, Kunming also became a top destination for foreigners wanting to live in China.

The more Kris and I pondered the idea of opening in Kunming, the more we realized the potential Kunming offered a business like ours. There were already plenty of Western cafés in Kunming – among them the Prague Café, French Café and Pizza da Rocco – but armed with home-made ice cream, an authentic Italian espresso machine and Mexican food, we had something new to offer.

We made a few exploratory trips to the city over the course of two months to look at possible locations for a new Salvador's. We hoped to find somewhere near Yunnan University as students are a good customer base for a café. The area around Wenlin Street between the university and Green Lake Park was already home to a large portion of Kunming's international community, and we knew that there was no better advertisement in China than foreign customers.

Wenlin Street is crossed by another small street called Wenhua Xiang, or "Culture Alley." Both streets are lined with six- to eight-story apartments with street-side storefronts underneath. Many of the businesses renting the storefronts in Wenhua Xiang were busy local restaurants and cafes that had converted single-story spaces into two-floor structures where customers had to duck to avoid hitting their heads.

The French Café and Prague Café had already established the neighborhood as Kunming's main area for foreign restaurants, and that was the market we wanted in on. The problem was that no one seemed to want to let go of their storefronts.

Over the next couple of months we made multiple trips to Kunming where Josh and Naoko let us stay with them. One night over dinner at their apartment, we began talking about how Kris and I would be able to manage two cafés – one in Dali and one in Kunming. The more we discussed it, the more Josh and Naoko took an interest, and soon we all realized how much easier things would be if we started a new partnership together. For me, I would have the best of both worlds. I would get to reap the benefits of expanding our business into a market far more stable than Dali's, and I would still get to live in Dali, the whole reason I still wanted to stay in China.

So we were a team of four, but we still had no space to open a Kunming location. We went through friends and agencies and followed every *For Rent* sign in the area, but all were dead ends. One day, after tea at the French Café, Josh and I took a stroll down Wenhua Xiang. We passed a Korean restaurant that had been open for about a year, and I asked Josh, "Have you ever seen a customer in there?" He shook his head. We stopped at the door and shrugged our shoulders. "It can't hurt to ask," I said.

There was no one at the door to greet us when we walked inside. We took a look around and found nothing but empty tables. Moments later, a woman on the second floor leaned over the railing and greeted us. I was expecting her to ask something like, "Two for lunch?" or, "Would you like to see our menu?" Instead she stunned us with the words, "Would you like to buy our business?"

CHAPTER 8

TO KILL A ROACH

The stench of rotten kimchee putrefied the air as Naoko stood motionless in the doorway. "I can't go back in there," she said with tears running down her face. "Fucking loaches everywhere." We knew what she meant. How could we not? Loaches or roaches, whatever one called them, were everywhere.

Two weeks after walking into that Korean restaurant for the first time, we made the decision to buy the four-year lease. We were the new tenants of 76 square meters of space just around the corner from the French Café. The location was perfect, but at a cost. Just for the privilege of owning the lease, we had to pay a one-time fee of about $13,000.

Somehow, on our two earlier visits, we failed to realize what a disaster the place was. The former owners had abandoned it in a revolting condition. They left open containers of unrefrigerated kimchee, a kind of Korean fermented cabbage, out in the kitchen which produced the kind of smell that would frighten even the most desensitized trash collector.

There were other problems too. The thin wooden dividing walls in the kitchen were rotten at the base and had deteriorated to a floppy mush. They wobbled like Jell-O when probed. One of the concrete walls had soaked through, spawning a dark creeping mold. White tile covered the rest of the kitchen walls and they were smothered in thick black oil. Years of frying oily Korean food without any ventilation had covered the wall with grime, which had hardened into an inch of indestructible surface oil. But far worse than any of that was that the future Salvador's Coffee House was home to thousands upon thousands of cockroaches.

Baby roaches crawled out from the CD player left behind by the former owners. Some floated upon the watery surface of the bowls of rotten kimchee – a sickening way to die. Roaches poured from the unplugged refrigerator, the cracks in the walls, the sinks and the power outlets. Roaches could be spotted on every square meter of floor or wall at any given time. They were fast, sneaky and knew all the best hiding places.

It was too late for second-guessing. The money had been handed over and the contract signed. The place was ours and we were not going to give it up just because of some damn bugs. We would have to gut the place, rip out the walls and bust off the wall tiles. Then we would destroy every last roach and start over from scratch.

On the first day of the extermination, Naoko hadn't made it but a few steps through the door before she burst into tears. The source of her dismay was the water cooler that we drank from the previous week when discussing the lease purchase with the former tenants. When she saw small roaches crawling out of the water spout her face went pale. The idea that this dump was to be her future was starting to sink in, and in a most unpleasant way.

Naoko wasn't the only one. All of us were questioning whether we had made a terrible mistake. But eventually we rolled up our sleeves and went on the offensive. We'd been discussing different tactical procedures for a while, but in the end, Josh opted for a combination of chemical warfare and brutal hands-on combat. He killed at least 15 from one extension cord.

One blast of roach spray – "loach splay," as Naoko called it – sent a shimmering mass of roaches running for their lives from the smallest cracks and crevices. In the kitchen, Kris lifted up a piece of plywood to find its other side covered with refugees. As the roaches scattered, so did we, kicking our knees in the air and screaming like frightened schoolchildren.

It was a hard-fought battle, but in the end, we were the victors. We eventually lost our fear of the roaches and had no trouble even squashing them with our bare hands. I'd always been of the philosophy that even roaches are living beings and should be respected as such, but in times of war, ethics became irrelevant. And that's really what it was – war. We were fighting for our investment and for our futures.

Josh, who had been a vegetarian most of his life and was known to avoid even harming insects, showed up every day with the look of a warrior. He wouldn't hesitate to use any means necessary, even if it meant crawling on his back under the grimy kitchen counters. When we would arrive in the morning, Josh looked like he'd already been in the trenches for hours.

By the end of it all we had become a well-oiled roach-killing machine. We'd spot movement five meters away and there was no way the little bugger would survive. We killed them all, and with little mercy, but the stench of rotten kimchee still lingered.

* * *

Our friend Wang Hu told us a Chinese saying: "If there are roaches in the kitchen, it means that the family is prosperous." His meaning was that the roaches were a good omen for our business. We weren't so sure about that, but we were glad that Wang Hu had come to help.

Wang Hu is a man of imposing stature. His thin goatee and serious countenance make him look like he could be cast as China's infamous Qin Emperor. In fact he was nothing like the cruel emperor. He was a talented artist and architect with a playful and passive demeanor, not the mafia boss one might assume.

Wang Hu was the child of two actors. His mother and father were relatively well-known performers in Shanghai before communist forces conquered the city. Wang Hu's grandfather had fought with Chiang Kai-Shek's Nationalist Party against the Japanese invasion, so once Mao's communist revolution took hold in the East, Wang Hu's mother and father were driven to Kunming with a fleeing nationalist army, supporting themselves by entertaining troops. When the communist revolution finally made it to Kunming in 1950, the Nationalist Party there was stamped out. Wang Hu's parents were then made to work as entertainers for the newly arrived communist army.

Wang Hu was born in Kunming in 1962 at the end of a four-year famine, known as the "Great Leap Forward", that took nearly 40 million lives across China. During the first four years of Wang Hu's childhood, his parents continued to perform as respected actors in Kunming and the family lived a relatively privileged life. Then the Cultural Revolution was launched and anything 'bourgeois' came under attack. Any possession of excess wealth, or even a higher education, was often enough to cause one to be fingered as a counter-revolutionary. In cities throughout China, no one was safe. Neighbors turned on neighbors, friends turned on friends, and even relatives turned on each other. Because Wang Hu's grandfather had previously been associated with the Nationalist Party, Wang Hu's father also became a victim of the witch hunt and he and his wife were sent to a labor camp outside of Kunming for re-education.

Wang Hu was then five years old. His two older brothers, aged 11 and 12, looked after him. The three had to fend for themselves in a city where many were starving. Families would sometimes fight each other to claim more food, and with their parents gone, the three brothers often got the short end of the stick. All meals were served in communal kitchens twice a day, but they were frequently left hungry and had to forage for wild foods on the hillsides out of town. Only during the short potato and corn harvests in spring and autumn were they able to eat their fill.

Forty years later, Wang Hu and his wife, Zhang Yunbin, were among Kunming's more respected architects.

"Wang Hu never really liked conventionality," Zhang Yunbin told me. "He was a free thinker, so the two of us together made for a good partnership. He would sketch out design ideas and I would plug them all into the computer to make them a reality."

We had first met Wang Hu and Zhang Yunbin in Dali when Kris and I opened the original Salvador's. It was after our victorious slaughter of the roaches that Wang Hu joined us for beers and offered us some remodeling tips.

Right from the beginning he disliked everything that the Korean restaurant owners had done. He eyed the workmanship with disdain and seemed to be muttering to himself, "It's wrong. It's all wrong." He went over to one of the tables and started sketching three-dimensional diagrams on a stack of napkins.

"The front bar windows should open like this," Wang Hu insisted, mimicking the movement of the car door on a DeLorean.

"But if they open like that, won't they be too heavy for our workers to lift?" Kris asked.

"You need to knock down this wooden frame and replace it with iron and glass," he continued.

"But if we do that, won't the bar have to move?" Josh asked.

"You need to add a spiral staircase made of wood and steel here," he went on.

"But won't that take up table space?" I asked.

Without even acknowledging our questions, Wang Hu handed over the napkin sketches, as if his work was done. We were skeptical of his ideas, but he had offered them for free, and people usually paid a small fortune for his services, so we were in no position to doubt his expertise.

One week later, Wang Hu's steel workers moved into the space and the structure quickly took shape. Wooden frames were sliced through diagonally with black steel beams that made Salvador's façade into a hybrid of steel and wood. The second floor windows were attached to eight vertically pivoting rods that supported eight panes of glass. The outside bar windows lifted up like the glass eyelashes of a giant robot.

By the end of July, the café was beginning to take shape and the major construction work was finished. Wang Hu's design provided us with a beautiful canvas on which we could decorate. We ripped out most of the wood framing and walls and replaced them with brick and concrete. Where possible, we used glass bricks to let some natural light pass through. Then we smashed an assortment of tiles into jagged pieces and cemented them into mixed mosaics. We used green tiles on the outside bar, black granite tiles on the inside bar and a mix of different colors and mirror fragments on the back wall of the ground floor.

The second floor had previously covered the same area as the ground floor, but this made the space feel cramped, so we ripped out the part of the second floor over the entryway to open things up. The Korean restaurant had previously used a beautiful chunk of hardwood for the sign with the restaurant's name, Koreana, carved upon it. We sanded it smooth and used it as our indoor bar top.

I have nothing but praise for Chinese workers when it comes to concrete, metal, glass or wood work, but when painting, they tend to throw paint around with little respect for straight lines. As my former boss in construction used to say, "There's nothing like a bad paint job to fuck up a whole room." So in between competitive games of Pacman on Josh's laptop, Josh, Naoko, Kris and I painted every square inch of the place ourselves.

We'd been warned many times that mixing business with friendship had risks. For the most part, I think we've proved them wrong. However, when it came to choices about lighting or paint colors, contention brewed.

In Dali, Kris and I had found that the stresses of designing the café resulted in some animated arguments, but then we had only been two partners. Now, however, the four of us had to reach some kind of agreement on every small decision, and when choosing the color for the structural beams we began yelling at each other in front of an uncomfortable paint salesman. Disagreements over the mosaic wall left two of us not speaking to each other, and even something as seemingly insignificant as deciding where to put the ice cream display threatened to tear our friendship apart.

This clash of personalities intensified with every step of the renovation. My own shortcomings also became more evident. There were times when my blood boiled just at the thought of not getting my way. I have a tendency to micromanage and over-think problems. The result is that I think I see things so clearly that I become overly opinionated. I thought I knew exactly what was needed to make Salvador's a functional restaurant with a design that would best serve our success, but I often failed to recognize the ideas of my partners.

Kris knew how I worked. He was used to my stubbornness and had learned to sway it or even use it against me when I started thinking things through in such detail that I overlooked the essentials. He too was opinionated, but he was always willing to work things out through calm debates.

My stubbornness, however, took a toll on Naoko's patience. She had communication issues from the beginning. Ls and Rs aside, her English was excellent. But when it came to arguing, her words often sounded malicious, or at least spiteful. I don't think she ever meant to offend, but there were times when her comments sent me into a silent rage. Although our disagreements were more superficial than substantive, they still planted the seeds of animosity.

Josh was an altogether different beast. His friendship with Kris and me and his marriage with Naoko often forced him into seeming disinterested in decision-making. He'd say he agreed with me when talking to me and he'd say he agreed with Kris when talking with Kris, and I could only assume that when he was alone with Naoko he agreed with her. He kept his true opinions to himself, which I found frustrating. I felt he was always telling me what I wanted to hear, which made it very difficult to move forward on serious decisions.

All four of us had previously shared a very close friendship, but the sad reality was that we would have to give up some of that in order to make our partnership work. Our differences manifested at more intense levels in future arguments over issues like pricing, operations and salary structuring, yet the arguments were essential to the evolution of our business.

Even with all the trouble it took to bring the Kunming Salvador's to completion, I can still say that it was also one of the most enjoyable times of my life. Remodeling a home or business in China can be frustrating when it comes to bargaining in wholesale markets or getting workers who do sub-par work. However, when it comes to fully customizing designs, China makes it easy – and at a far lower cost.

Just around the corner from our future restaurant was a glass cutter who could follow any design we gave him. Another block over was the metalworker who custom-built all of our iron and stainless steel tables, as well as the shelving to fit our oddly shaped kitchen. A family of wood workers from Sichuan living in Dali built all of our tables and chairs from walnut wood. We could sketch any idea we had out on paper and the craftsmen and craftswomen would make it happen.

There is nothing quite like the feeling that comes from bringing life to something that was once lifeless. For us, that is what remodeling Salvador's Coffee House in Kunming was like. We took to the construction as an artist would when painting an enormous canvas – we'd have to step back every once in a while to make sure our composition made sense of colors and spacing.

On August 3rd, my 27th birthday, we took a break on our new bean bags on the second floor and admired our work. Though rather bare, the space felt right. Wang Hu's signature metal and glass design melded well with our more classic approach to colors and arrangement. We'd spent quite a bit of the past month arguing over designs, but in the end we were all pretty happy.

Then Kris's phone rang.

"You're not gonna believe this," Kris said to me, intense disappointment evident in both his tone of voice and the saddened look in his eyes. "They're kicking us out. We're losing the Dali Salvador's."

There are few people in this world I despise more than our former Dali landlords. The husband was bad enough, with his sinister grin and oily black hair. But the thought of that woman with her beehive hairstyle, dangly earrings and slobbish figure made my blood boil. She had a "black heart like a lump of coal oozing tar," Kris was once angry enough to say to her face.

They tricked us. It was the cinema and disco ordeal all over again, but this time we weren't just losing a contract, we were losing everything we'd put into the Dali Salvador's. Less than a year earlier, we had signed a three-year contract with our landlords – who already knew that the place was slated for demolition a year later. They signed their names and stamped their fingerprints, assuring us three years at a fixed rent – but the contract meant nothing once the demolition crews arrived.

I had never planned to move to Kunming, and I don't think I would even have considered living in China if it were not for Dali. Most of my friends were in Dali, and I'd become accustomed to Dali's easy-going lifestyle where the most difficult choices each day revolved around where to eat. Dali was a place where the air was clean and fresh, where we could ride a horse cart out to the big grass field to play Frisbee or soccer, and where we'd finish each day at the Bird Bar, whiskey in hand. Kunming had none of that and I had no desire to live there.

If the landlords had given us the news three months earlier, before the Kunming plan had started taking shape, it probably would have been enough to send us packing. We hadn't really saved any money yet and it would have been time to give up in China and head back home to wait tables in someone else's restaurant. But as we sat there in our bean bags, tears in our eyes, there was still reason to be optimistic about the future of Salvador's. We were losing something very valuable to us in Dali, but we knew this would not be the end of our pursuits. We were really just getting started. My home would have to be wherever Salvador's went, and I would have to find a way to leave Dali behind.

One month after opening in Kunming, Kris and I returned to Dali for one last "hoorah" at our flagship business. All of our old friends were there and we partied like it was the end of the world. We tore out everything and even removed all of the glass windows and doors to give to our friendly glass recycler – we didn't want the landlords to make a penny off of anything.

Toward the end of the night we started smashing everything out of pure hedonistic pleasure. The police were called because of noise complaints, but when hearing what the landlords had done to us, they let us carry on. It was a memorable party with all of our Dali friends, but for me it was also a mournful goodbye to a place that I thought I would forever call home.

CHAPTER 9

TRAVELING CIRCUS

M r. Li was a pudgy and awkward looking man with a facial tick that always made him look like he was biting into something sour. "Nobody has ever started a Wholly Foreign Owned Enterprise with such a small investment," he told us. "The last one we permitted was well over $100,000." This was discouraging news considering our total investment barely topped $30,000.

A Wholly Foreign Owned Enterprise (WFOE – commonly referred to as a "woofie") would allow us to be legitimate business owners in China. This was a designation that had in the past been off limits to foreigners unless they were part of larger companies. New regulations, however, allowed foreigners to start up small companies without needing Chinese business partners as long as the investment amount was sufficient.

In Dali, we were secret owners of Salvador's. All the paperwork was in our friend's name. We had no legal rights to operate the business and we lived in China on tourist visas. But the visa rules were changing, and to retain the tourist visas we would have to travel across southern China to Hong Kong every three months to renew. The woofie could make life easier by granting us a 10-year company license with yearly work visas for all four of us. Thanks to the government connections of Wang Hu and Zhang Yunbin, we were granted meetings with Mr. Li. He alone had the power to grant us the woofie.

It's no secret that in Chinese business dealings, bribery of some sort is often the easiest path to securing licensing and other government support. The culture of *guanxi*, connections built upon reciprocity, is still a big part of getting things done in China. "Gifts" are the means to build government connections. Cigarettes, liquor and cash-filled red envelopes known as *hongbao* are the traditional *guanxi* builders. But this can be a slippery slope as the price for cooperation can rise quickly.

Naoko had a different strategy. She approached every official empty-handed, bringing only her smile. She offered them friendship instead of goods. This kind of *guanxi* proved far more durable than any that could have been purchased.

Most Chinese still begrudge the Japanese for the brutality inflicted upon the country during Japan's invasion in World War II. Naoko had been a victim of this prejudice more than a few times, but with her friendly and polite demeanor and her fluent Chinese, government officials took an immediate liking to her. With three Americans in tow who could also speak Chinese, we were a spectacle that stirred everyone's curiosity. They'd often let us bypass lines of other waiting applicants just to see what we were all about. Kris loved this kind of attention and would often one-up the entertainment with juggling or gymnastics demonstrations. At times we felt more like a traveling circus than entrepreneurs.

Mr. Li took a special liking to Naoko. Her Chinese was better than ours, and everyone seemed to marvel at her proficiency. Over the span of a month, Naoko and Mr. Li laid the groundwork for our woofie. The remodeling was nearly done and once we had the license we'd be ready to open the doors for business. The agreement was that, for our investment, we would be granted the company title, Kunming Salvador's Food and Beverage Company, Limited. Our business would be protected under law and the unfortunate series of events that led to losing our Dali business would not be repeated in Kunming.

We walked into Mr. Li's office one August afternoon expecting to walk out with the approval for our woofie.

"All the paperwork looks good," said Mr. Li, "So now what you need to do is transfer your $30,000 into a government account. Then, as you spend it, you will need valid receipts that show how the money was spent."

Naoko's jaw dropped. Kris's face went pale. Josh buried his eyes in the palms of his hands.

While Naoko and Mr. Li discussed the details of what he meant by the money transfer, Josh, Kris and I had a little side conversation about how screwed we were. We were practically ready to open and we'd already spent all of the money. Mr. Li was telling us that before we spent the money, it needed to go through a government-regulated investment account. Moreover, we would need to valid receipts to account for all of the spent funds – we had not collected any.

In China, there are two kinds of receipts. There are the valid receipts known as *fapiao* that are recorded by the tax department, and there are the handwritten ones that stay secret and never get taxed. If you ask for *fapiao* when making purchases, many businesses will charge you up to 15 percent more to cover the cost of issuing them. We were on a tight budget when buying equipment and supplies, so we always opted for the handwritten receipts. Without a time a machine to go back and un-spend our money, we appeared to be in trouble.

Naoko and Mr. Li spent the next hour discussing how we would have to find another $30,000, transfer it into an out-of-country bank account and then transfer it again to the Kunming government account. We had spent all of our money, some of it borrowed, to build Salvador's. We had nothing left.

Next we had to go back to every single place we'd paid for goods and services for renovating the new Salvador's and collect *fapiao*. We had made purchases in dozens of places throughout Kunming and even in faraway coastal cities like Guangzhou and Shanghai. In order to replace handwritten receipts with *fapiao* we had to cover the cost of each company's taxes. It took us six months to account for all $30,000 with *fapiao* before we could pay back Wang Hu and Zhang Yunbin.

In the end, it was worth all of the trouble. We were finally legitimate business owners, something that wouldn't have been possible without Naoko's tenacity. She proved to us just how valuable she was.

Naoko sweet-talked her way through each obstacle and achieved what most said was impossible – a legitimate small business in China owned by foreigners. Originally, Naoko hadn't even been considered a potential partner – it was only going to be Josh, Kris and me – but to leave her out would have been a terrible mistake. Without the license, our business would be unsustainable, and in some ways illegal, and without Naoko it would have been very difficult to get the license.

The company license was only one of many hurdles ahead of us. In dealing with the Health and Sanitation Department, the Fire and Safety Department, the Environmental Department, the Foreign Investment Department, the Public Safety Bureau and the National and Provincial Tax Departments, obstacles proved even more formidable, but Naoko took on all of the meetings and paperwork with a certain charm that swayed notoriously difficult officials to our side.

Finally, one day in late August, Naoko walked into Salvador's beaming with pride. She held our company license up for all of us to see. "Tomorrow," she said, "I'm going to get this flamed." We were pretty sure we knew what she meant, but we hid all the matches anyway.

CHAPTER 10

ICE CREAM DIPLOMACY

If chivalry is truly dead, Qin Hui tries his best to resurrect it in Kunming.

Every morning he mounts his trusty steed – a well-traveled red electric scooter – and ventures off into the city. Somehow he manages to steer while eating an apple with one hand and answering his incessantly-ringing phone with the other. If someone crosses him along his quest, Qin Hui will unsheathe a verbal thrashing. "Dirt hooligan" or "dog dick" is likely to be accompanied by apple shrapnel spraying from his lips. Drivers beware: Qin Hui wields a sharp tongue and he's not afraid to use it.

Qin Hui is a handsome man with a strong build who always sports freshly-buzzed short hair. He zips around Kunming running more errands every day than most could manage in a week. These days, many of the errands are for Salvador's, but he has never shied away from helping countless others who seek out his special set of skills.

Whether it was clearing out construction garbage, finding a woodworker, fixing electrical problems, sourcing ingredients, or even helping foreigners get their visas, Qin Hui could do it all, and always with a smile and a sharp whistle. He whistled to say hi, he whistled to say bye, and often he even whistled for no apparent reason at all.

Qin Hui came from a small village about twelve kilometers from Xuanwei, one of Yunnan's most productive coal towns. He grew up tending the family pigs and cows, but he escaped family responsibilities as often as possible to get out on his bicycle. In those days, his bicycle was his most treasured possession, and even though he lived at school, he often skipped class to ride out to the other villages or down to Xuanwei.

"I got around everywhere as a kid," Qin Hui told me. "By the time I was 14, everyone within a 20 kilometer radius knew who I was."

In 1992, Qin Hui moved to Kunming and found work at the Yunnan train wheel factory. He became an assistant to the boss, running errands for him and dealing with simple repairs. After working there for six years he joined his brother at an apartment complex and served as a security guard. This was about the same time that Manu and Lotta moved into Qin Hui's building.

Manu and Lotta, owners of the French Café, were Qin Hui's first foreign friends. Qin Hui had always been fascinated by foreigners but had never really met any, so any problems Manu and Lotta had with their apartment, Qin Hui would jump at the chance to help out.

One day the couple had a problem with a leaky pipe and they asked Qin Hui if they knew a good plumber. Qin Hui insisted that he could handle it himself. He showed up wearing a raincoat and carrying a few wrenches in his hand. He then crawled under the sink and removed a connection to the main line. Water sprayed everywhere while he removed the pipe. The kitchen was drenched but Qin Hui stayed dry under his jacket, laughing with glee the entire time.

Qin Hui eventually earned a reputation as a kind of 'fixer' for many of the foreigners who had made Kunming their home. He was the man to ask for anything from finding a new apartment to getting a washing machine fixed. In fact, he was so helpful that in those early days, many theorized he must have been some sort of government spy tasked with infiltrating Kunming's foreign community. This was, of course, not true – he was just an incredibly selfless individual with no ulterior motives – but many were suspicious about what would make someone so helpful.

Qin Hui approached each favor as a way to build up friendships and connections, and he was always eager to meet new people. Sometimes this paid off for him when he received cash gifts during Chinese New Year, but favors often went unreciprocated.

Qin Hui was with us at Salvador's in Kunming from the very beginning. I first met him when he delivered food for us to a friend's house. I was visiting for lunch, and found it strange that someone would carry our food up eight flights to the apartment since Kunming didn't have a food delivery service. Moreover, the man seemed dressed far nicer than any delivery man I'd ever known. My friends explained that Qin Hui basically ran everything in their apartment complex from security and parking to repairs and maintenance. He had even offered to deliver food to my friends whenever they didn't feel like leaving the apartment.

Qin Hui was instrumental during construction and even helped Kris and I find our own apartments. He was tenacious, hardworking and motivated, and sometimes it felt like we were wasting his talents on menial tasks, but he seemed to take pleasure just in the act of helping. The problem was that we weren't the only ones getting his help. His phone rang incessantly with others in the neighborhood seeking him out to fix their own problems. We wanted to make sure he continued to work for us, so we started giving him a full-time salary.

At one point, Naoko was getting so bogged down with licensing paperwork, she thought maybe she could try and give Qin Hui some of the tasks. He was from the countryside, so we worried that he might be a little 'too country' to relate well with cranky government officials. But Qin Hui would show up at an official's office, mouth full of sunflower seeds, and talk to them like they were old friends. He could relate to anybody, and he had a gift for finding ways to connect with people that he was meeting for the first time.

When friendship wasn't enough, Qin Hui would use our homemade ice cream to get through more difficult bureaucratic obstacles. Our all-natural ice cream had earned a favorable reputation in Kunming, and Qin Hui utilized this fact as a kind of 'ice cream diplomacy.' With ice cream in hand, he quickly made more friends in just about every government department. Moreover, those very same officials often found their own way to Salvador's, sometimes with their children in tow, to get a little more of that ice cream.

Qin Hui was one of many who were instrumental to getting our company set up and the business running. With him and all of the other connections we made in those first few months, we were finally able to open the doors to our fully-licensed business.

The four of us had invested everything we had for the Kunming Salvador's and it was up to the people of Kunming to decide what happened next.

Above: Colin's first trip to Asia.
Below: Colin and Josh on a motorcycle trip in China.

Left: Aling with her parents and sister. Below: Tributary of Three Gorges on the Yangtze River.

Left: Village progress prospect at Bangdong School. Below: A family yurt in Xinjiang.

Above: Colin and Kris in front of their first business in Dali. Left: Salvador's staff in Kunming.

Opposite top: Newspaper clipping about the bomber. Opposite bottom: Salvador's staff on rock climbing day.

谴责暴行

65 分钟公交两劫难

公交车爆炸

7 月 21 日,昆明市两辆 54 路公交车先后在客运站台和人民西路路口发生爆炸案,造成 2 名乘客死亡,14 名乘客不同程度受伤。

7 月 22 日本报版面

疑犯 李彦

多警种全力侦查
文化巷洋咖啡吧爆炸

文化巷爆炸

12 月 25 日本报版面

震惊全国的昆明 "7·21" 公交爆炸案终于宣布告破!

圣诞前夕发生在文化巷的咖啡屋爆炸案同样成功告破!

都

疑犯厌世报复

为什么死者就是嫌疑人?

记者刘晶晶 黄米娜 昨天下午 4 时许,昆明市公安局召开新闻发布会,副市长、市公安局局长边赫敏向媒体发布了今年两起爆炸案全部告破的消息。

大量证据证明,正是 12 月 24 日萨尔瓦多咖啡屋爆炸案与两起公交车爆炸案性质一样...

关经过大量的调查取证工作,证实这两起案件并非像传言中的微恐怖活动有关...

面对近 50 家媒体,伍路说...

此时,杜建已近 30 小时没睡觉...

警方的通报内容也让在坐的记者与市民心中的疑团一个个迎刃而解。

疑犯厌世报复

记者:听完整个新闻通报,案件比较明朗...

记者:现在已经证明了两起案件的犯罪嫌疑人是李彦,那么能否再次确认其是否是医护人员。

杜:不是,是医护人员...

Left: Kris on his head.
Below: First day meeting Kris.

Opposite top: Shifu at Wuwei Temple, Dali.
Opposite bottom: Zhang Yunbin and Wang Hu.

Left: A mountain village girl with her grandmother.
Below: Visiting the family of an employee in a mountain village.

CHAPTER 11

RAISING DUCKS

Aling grew up in a small village in Dehong Prefecture near the border with Myanmar. Fields of sugarcane blanket the flat expanse at the edge of the mountainous border. They rustle with the same rhythm of a soft rain as the smell of fermenting cane wafts along with the morning fog from the nearby sugar refinery.

When Aling's parents first moved to the village in 1983 from the mountains to the east, western Yunnan was a much less populated and wilder place. There were tribal conflicts where the Chinese government rarely dared to intervene. Thick jungles lined much of the border area of China and Myanmar and wild animals were still plentiful – family legend has it that Aling's great-aunt was actually killed by a pack of wolves. When China's central government made maneuvers to firm up its borders with Myanmar, incentives were given to farmers willing to move along the border towns. Forests were cleared for sugarcane and other crops, and the wilderness disappeared.

Aling's family raised a flock of more than 200 ducks. From the age of 10 it was her responsibility to walk the ducks from the farmhouse to a pond on the other side of the valley to feed off the small fish and insects that lived there. She would carry a long bamboo stick with a crinkly plastic bag tied to the end of it that would frighten them into order whenever one stepped out of line or started nibbling on other farmers' rice plants. She would have to count them over and over again just to make sure no stragglers evaded her watch.

At night her family kept the ducks penned up next to the stilted house, but up on the first floor of the open-air home, they kept about 20 rabbits. On some nights, as the pigs back in the pen behind the house grunted their last sighs of the day, Aling would fall asleep holding in her arms as many rabbits as she could.

Aling never had time for school as she had to help take care of her younger sister while her parents worked in the cane fields. Even when only four years old, Aling carried her sister everywhere with her on her back in a tightly wrapped cloth stitched with colorful patterns.

When the sisters grew older, they hiked together in the nearby hills collecting bamboo grubs and wasp larvae to sell to vendors in town. Sometimes wasp stings would make their eyes swell shut and their lips puff up, but the insects were delicacies that could be sold to traders at a high price. The two young girls were willing to take on the stings if it meant making some extra money for the family.

During harvest season, Aling helped her mother trim the long leaves from the towering cane, and later chop them down to sell to the sugar factory. When Aling was 12, her father leased a new property in a nearby village where he planted kumquat trees in hopes of bringing in more money for the family. For the most part, his kumquat venture proved successful, but with each passing day he would come home later and later and was often in a terrible mood.

What Aling's family didn't know was that her father was taking his earnings into town to spend on lottery tickets. His gambling soon turned into an uncontrollable addiction. The more he lost, the more lottery tickets he bought in a hopeless attempt to recoup his losses. His luck never changed, and Aling watched him lose everything he had worked for. Her once devoted father slowly became a different person – one she no longer looked up to.

Aling's family had lived a simple life, a life where everyone was provided for and no one ever went hungry, but as her father's gambling addiction worsened, they often found themselves sleeping on empty stomachs. Sometimes Aling and her sister went to grave sites to try and scavenge food and other offerings left by family members of the deceased just to get something to quell their hunger. At one point her sister even developed skin sores and bumps on her body from malnutrition. Neighbors loaned the family cured pork just to make sure she ate enough over the winter season.

At age 14, Aling wanted nothing more to do with her father and his continued irresponsible behavior. She woke up early one morning, packed a bag with a couple of changes of clothes and told her parents that she was leaving to find work in the city. She had only 23 yuan ($3) in her pocket and had to spend half of it on that first bus ride out of town.

At first no one would hire Aling because of her young age, but eventually she found work in a factory that made floorboards out of wood shipped from Myanmar. She had been there for about six months when a stack of floorboards collapsed and lacerated two of her fingers. It wasn't a very serious injury, but the factory decided that she was too young for the job.

She then found a new job at a small restaurant where she cleaned and washed dishes. The owners were kind to her and taught her how to cook. She stayed with them for about a year until one day she saw the owner kill and butcher a dog. It wasn't a surprise to her that the restaurant served dog meat as it was a featured menu item, but it was the first time she had seen one of the animals butchered. She swore never again to eat dog meat and decided that she could no longer work at the restaurant.

Aling had been away from home for two years when the price of sugarcane suddenly skyrocketed. Workers came down from their mountain villages to find work with the farmers who were scrambling to capitalize on the market boom. Aling too found work at one of the migrant camps as a cook. It was there that she realized she had a natural talent for cooking.

For the next few years she changed jobs many times to work at different restaurants, learning as much as she could. In 2004, five years after leaving home, she took a 10-hour bus ride to Dali to search out new work and new cooking experiences. This brought her to a 'Help Wanted' sign posted on the door of Salvador's Coffee House.

Aling walked through the front door, went up to the counter and asked our manager, Mengjuan, about applying for the job. Mengjuan gave her a skeptical glance and pointed her towards my table. Aling was wearing a tight black T-shirt with styled slits cut into it along the arms, back and belly, revealing her dark brown skin beneath. She approached as an old friend would, uninhibited and seemingly devoid of any apprehension. She was different from the other applicants, who usually cowered in the presence of a foreigner and nervously avoided making any direct eye contact.

I found her demeanor and appearance alluring, and when she sat down in the chair opposite me, I'm sure I blushed. Seeing through my awkwardness, she smiled knowingly. But soon we were chatting about her past work experience and what her responsibilities at Salvador's would be. Kris arrived moments later and we agreed to hire her.

The first week was frustrating for Aling as Mengjuan and our other new workers adjusted to living together. But with Aling's natural talents in the kitchen, she soon proved to be an excellent worker. She was also very sociable with the customers. At times, however, she was overly brash and did not take criticism too well. She had a fiery personality that some of the girls initially found off-putting. But after the first month, Aling settled into her new job.

On one occasion, Kris and I noticed Aling scribbling cartoonish drawings on a note pad when she took orders. When we questioned her about this, we learned that she had never attended school and had never learned to read or write. Instead she had invented her own written language of spirals, crosses and pictograms. It was a language that only she could read, but it served her well enough in the restaurant.

When we made the move to Kunming, Aling played an important role in structuring the new kitchen. Our menu grew to include more breakfasts, sandwiches, Mexican foods, salads and pastas, all of which

Aling learned quickly, and she asserted herself as a mentor for the new employees.

Over the course of our first year in Kunming, our business grew to be about five times that of the Dali restaurant. Our staff increased to 12, and Josh, Naoko, Kris and I learned to give more and more responsibilities over to the girls. Though Aling was exceptional in the kitchen, her illiteracy made accounting work challenging. So, as Mengjuan worked her way up to commanding the register behind the bar, Aling earned her spot as a kitchen manager. They both still rotated among kitchen and waitressing positions, but also took on responsibilities that extended beyond their shifts.

In her new role as kitchen manager, I often had private meetings with Aling to discuss employee grievances and new ideas to improve kitchen efficiency. I took her on walks in the park to discuss schedules, but instead we fed breadcrumbs to the birds at the lake. We had lunch meetings to discuss new menu items, but instead we talked about our childhoods. With each meeting, I found myself more and more attracted to her, but, as I had done many times in my life, I pushed aside any feelings for her. Dating an employee seemed irresponsible and inappropriate, and I was afraid of making her uncomfortable and causing her to leave.

By strange coincidence, Aling and I shared the same birthday, August 3rd. Nearly one year after opening in Kunming, we closed the restaurant down to celebrate our birthdays together with co-workers and friends. I was turning 27 and Aling was turning 20. Beer flowed, and soon all of us were red-faced and slurring. Throughout the evening, there were a number of times when Aling would catch my furtive glance, and sometimes I'd catch hers. It became obvious that we were fighting a losing battle against our self-control. We sent flirtatious text messages back and forth for a couple of weeks, until we ultimately caved in to our desires.

At first we kept our relationship secret from our friends and co-workers, as we were concerned that it might have negative consequences. But it didn't take long for people to figure things out. For the most part, our friends were supportive, but working together became increasingly awkward, and Aling decided to quit her job at Salvador's and move in with me. We took in a puppy – one that looked more like a fluffy black muppet than a dog – and Aling named him *Hei Hei*, "Black Black."

Soon after leaving Salvador's, Aling began to pursue her own business ideas. She bought a foot-pumped sewing machine and started designing custom handbags made from colorful Burmese fabrics. She then expanded her business to include custom jewelry made from stones and recycled copper wire. This evolved into her own brand of jewelry and art called *Xiao Hei Dao*, "Little Black Island."

Aling had grown up in a world full of color. When not at home tending to the many animals on her farm, she would venture into other neighboring villages. Many who lived in her village were of the Dai minority – an ethnicity in Yunnan known for spicy foods and vibrant patterned fabrics. When just a child, Aling would spend the night with local Dai families in their elevated bamboo homes. They would teach her local recipes and include her in their holidays and festivals or take her out into the farmlands and forests surrounding the village. Her daily life alone was enough to have her mind racing with artistic inspiration, but before coming to Kunming she never had the opportunity to put color to canvas.

In Kunming, Aling developed a unique style of art where she cut up colorful Burmese fabrics left over from the handbag production. She would stick these pieces onto canvases using glue that she made by herself from sticky rice. The strips of fabric were delicately pieced together to create works that ranged from abstract renditions of village life to surreal mindscapes that came to her in dreams. She took to her new profession with natural ingenuity and aptitude, and soon made a name for herself in Kunming as the spunky artist from the countryside.

It was amazing to watch her. She had never attended an art class of any sort, but once inspired there was nothing to get in the way of her success. Aling was by all measures special. She was talented, beautiful, smart and incredibly personable. I'm confident that even if Aling never walked in through the door of Salvador's, she would have found a way to express herself. However, there is little doubt that her move to the city brought about opportunities that would not have been available to her back in the village.

Village life does not offer the most welcoming atmosphere to individual pursuits, and most village women fall into their roles as obedient daughters, wives and mothers. If there is one thing positive I can say with certainty about urban life in China, it is that it opens the doors of personal freedom to those who might not otherwise have it. Cities have an atmosphere that stimulates self-expression, and for Aling, this fact helped launch her career.

This was the essence of the ongoing migration from China's countryside. It was something very different from the forced urbanization I had witnessed more than five years earlier at the Three Gorges Dam site. Money was one reason people abandoned their farms, but for many it was also a chance to be something more than they could back in the village. For women especially, it was a chance to be empowered beyond the role they were expected to play at home.

This fact was never lost on me or my business partners. We knew that all of the girls that left their families behind to work with us were hoping to find more than just a steady salary. They hoped to discover their own potential, and it was our responsibility to help them find it.

CHAPTER 12

The Republic of Salvador's

As many in the business would attest, it takes more than making good food and creating an appetizing ambiance to make a restaurant profitable. The biggest challenges come from designing and instituting effective operations. Not only did we need to staff the restaurant, but we needed to find a way to make it run efficiently and profitably, while maintaining a safe and clean environment.

Salvador's has a large and complicated menu, with fresh coffees, homemade ice creams, baked goods, breakfasts, Mexican food, Italian food and a full bar. All of our employees came from the countryside. They had no experience with anything on the Salvador's menu, and certainly had never dealt with foreigners before. So for our business to succeed, we had to run things a bit differently.

Business in Dali had been slow and simple with only three employees. Everyone could do every job so no real specialization was necessary. But in Kunming we needed two shifts of bakers, cooks, dishwashers and food runners. Because the girls who already worked for us had experience with all of these jobs, it seemed senseless to distinguish who was to be baker, cook or any of the other jobs. So with the addition of five new employees, we created a system where everyone alternated among all the jobs. This meant that the person who was baker one week might be waitress the next week, dishwasher the following, then cook, and so forth.

The obvious drawback to this approach was that we didn't have any single professional cook or baker. Instead, we had many. This meant that our dishes fluctuated depending upon who happened to be in the kitchen that day. Some made bagels wide and some made them tall. Some made moist, chewy cookies and some made them dry and crumbly. Some had a knack for baking but weren't the best at making foamy cappuccinos. But we felt there were far more advantages to the system than disadvantages. One was that we were able to schedule a day off each week for every employee. In China, people in the service industry rarely, if ever, get paid days off; but we wanted well-rested and energized employees who had time to live their lives outside of work.

I had worked in four different restaurants in Colorado, and in each one there was a wall of contempt between the kitchen and the dining area. Restaurant wait staff were blamed by cooks if orders were ill-timed, and wait staff blamed kitchens if orders took too long. Cooks grumbled about wait staff making so much in tips from their work in the kitchen, and wait staff complained about poorly prepared food. This usually created a barrier that few restaurants ever successfully bridged.

At Salvador's, every girl was empowered with skills to do every job in the restaurant, and this generated a kind of understanding for each other's work. For example, the cook was a little more patient with the waitress who messed up an order, because she herself had likely made similar mistakes. The girls were thus able to monitor each other's mistakes and double-check the quality of each other's food preparation and customer service. On some weeks the dishwasher was actually more experienced with food preparation than the cook, so she could tell the chef that the Alfredo sauce needed more cream, or that the salsa wasn't spicy enough. Such input from a dishwasher would be considered outrageous in a typical restaurant, but it continually improved each girl's skills, and it bonded them with a shared desire to make Salvador's better.

One problem with the system, however, was that even though it was designed to empower all employees equally, there were hierarchical tendencies among the girls. This was most evident in our monthly group meetings where usually only the girls who had been there the longest spoke out about problems and new ideas. Newer girls often said nothing, feeling it inappropriate to speak up because of how far down the ladder they were. We tried to circumvent this problem by conducting one-on-one meetings with each employee.

In these meetings I found that even the shyest and least participatory members of the group meetings would share some of the most revealing grievances and innovative ideas. For them, it was an opportunity to offer their own thoughts about running the kitchen, improving customer service or even improving health and safety standards. For each girl to have the opportunity to speak privately and freely with her boss gave them all a chance to think critically about every part of the business, even when it came to criticism of me and the other owners.

Village girls in China are often raised to be obedient to their parents – and then obedient to their husbands – with little respect for their own personal ambitions. When Kris first met A Li's parents back when A Li and Kris worked together at the Sunshine Café, A Li's mother told Kris that as her boss he should smack her whenever she gets out of line. We, of course, never smacked any of our employees – though we continue to receive playful beatings from them on a daily basis. When A Li's mother said that to Kris, she was essentially saying that he was now her guardian.

We never took our eyes off the business, but the health and happiness of the Salvador's girls also became a priority. Their lives became intertwined with our own, and we increasingly resembled a family. This made for a very special work environment, and required a special approach to how we operated.

Josh, Naoko, Kris and I altogether have six brothers and no sisters. With the growing number of girls we employed at Salvador's, we began to learn a bit about what it's like to have sisters. We teased them and they teased us. If we made one angry, she might not speak to us for a week, or until one of us apologized. We became more involved in their lives and we'd worry about the boys they dated. If not having a sister in one's life is considered a deficiency, the Salvador's girls were our prescription for completeness.

"You can't be friends with your workers," one local friend told us. It was advice we never heeded. It would never work for us to run a business in China the same as Chinese do, just as it would never work for us to run a Western-style business with Chinese employees. So we ran things differently from everyone else and we were proud of it. We fully embraced our family approach and did everything possible to strengthen it.

We would close Salvador's one day every other month for team-building trips with our staff. We went rock climbing, bowling, grass skiing and fruit picking. We went to hot springs, yoga class, parks, employee weddings in the countryside, mini golf, first aid training, picnics and many dinners together. These outings helped everyone know each other better outside of the work environment and further functioned to oil the cogs of our operational machine.

Employment benefits at Salvador's also included free room and board, private English tutoring, paid vacations, health insurance and profit sharing. Providing employees with free room and board is actually very common in China, especially in the restaurant business. Migrant workers from the countryside are a lot easier to find if their living expenses are covered.

A number of our customers were foreigners who taught at nearby high schools and universities. Many were proficient in Chinese and often joined us at the evening employee meal. Eventually, we had the idea that customers like these could teach the girls English in three one-hour private lessons each week in exchange for free unlimited food and drink. The going rate for native English-speaking tutors was about 100 yuan (about $12.50) per hour, so as long as tutors consumed more than 300 yuan of food and drink each week, it was a good deal for them. Of course, because our costs for the food and drink were far lower than the retail price, it was also a good deal for us. More importantly, it was an invaluable bonus for our employees.

Employees initially received English lessons based off of our menu in order to learn the essentials of taking orders in English, but the tutoring also contributed to the girls' development as adults. Girls often started at

Salvador's as young as 16. For most of them, coming to work at Salvador's was not only their first time working in a restaurant, but their first time away from their village. They started at Salvador's with little experience of being independent and so were wary of everything and everyone at Salvador's. It was always a difficult transition for the first few months as they tried to keep up with the more experienced girls.

Everything was new to them. Coffee was a strange bitter tea. Mexican food was something they'd never tried before – many had never even heard of Mexico. Cheese was an odd substance, feta cheese especially, and not something they would ever want to introduce to their palates. While new employees started private English lessons soon after their arrival, most of them had never even seen a foreigner other than on television, and they most definitely had never talked to one. The English lessons offered this opportunity.

For the first time in their lives, the girls sat down at a table with a foreigner and had a conversation. The English lessons soon turned their timidity into confidence. They smiled more, became more playful and generally looked happier.

The tutoring program was valuable to the girls even after their lives moved beyond Salvador's Coffee House. Education for their children means everything to most Chinese parents, and though Salvador's English tutoring was far from the education that they may have envisioned, it was significant in its own way. We got applicants every week from many who held high school diplomas, sometimes even college degrees. They wanted to work for us free of charge just for the opportunity to practice their English. We turned them away nearly every time for a number of reasons, but mainly because we knew that they would not be able to keep up with the hard work of our other employees.

Workers from the countryside were instrumental in Kunming's urbanization throughout the first decade of this century. Migrant workers were not afraid of hard work and could be paid lower salaries than those from the city. When most in the West think of factory work in China, they envision sweatshops where people slave long hours under horrible conditions with little pay. But the truth is that most workers who migrate to the city from the countryside are there by choice and see any kind of employment as an opportunity to climb the socioeconomic ladder from countryside farmer to urban middle class. Even though employment might mean long hours and hard work, urban employers manage to find a balance to provide just enough to attract migrant laborers from the poorer countryside. So as atrocious as some working conditions may seem to outsiders, many migrants see this kind of employment as an opportunity, not a curse.

From an early age, village girls learn quickly to shoulder many of their family's responsibilities. They cook, they clean and they tend to the farm and the farm animals. Once they reach the age of about 22, they are expected to add mothering to their duties. There is rarely room for personal aspirations. For boys, it is usually different as they have fewer responsibilities at home and more freedom to pursue goals that take them away from mundane family duties.

When village girls leave the countryside to find work in the city, they are already equipped for hard work. They tend to be more responsible than many of the males who pursue work in the city as they are already accustomed to managing the village household. This often makes them excellent employees but also leaves them vulnerable to mistreatment. At Salvador's we tried our best to break this mold by empowering the girls who came to work for us with a safe and healthy work environment and opportunities that extended beyond it.

A major concern for migrant workers is the availability of basic health care, both for themselves and for their families back home. Though villagers have been minimally covered by a rural insurance program, serious medical conditions require treatments at city-level hospitals which often put families deep in debt. When villagers move to the city they lose their rural insurance coverage, so our employees always arrived uninsured.

At Salvador's, Josh and Naoko were always there to answer medical questions or provide treatment when needed. This service was invaluable, as Josh and Naoko were qualified to give the girls free medical advice and/or treatment, and often even extended this to include their family members. If further medical attention was needed, Josh and Naoko could connect them with trustworthy doctors or clinics throughout the city.

Along with these educational, health and other employee benefits, we eventually added profit sharing into the mix. This led to what I see as one of our greatest accomplishments – handing the reins over to the girls. Once the girls knew that, in a small way, they were in charge of their own salaries, they took an entirely different approach to their work. If Salvador's made more money, so would they. Suddenly they were all finding ways to make the restaurant more efficient and more enjoyable for customers.

When Kris worked at Sunshine Café back in Dali, the girls who worked with him were only paid 250 yuan ($30) per month. He was getting paid nearly 10 times that much and never felt very good about it. The girls were taking on the hardest jobs, but they were barely making ends meet. Kris always tried his best to right this inequality by sharing his own salary and bonuses.

At Salvador's, we brought this same sense of equality to the business, and profit sharing turned out to be one of the best investments we ever made. After our first four years at the Kunming Salvador's, it became apparent that the girls could more or less run things on their own. Responsibilities that Josh, Naoko, Kris and I had originally taken increasingly shifted to become theirs. They even earned the ability to decide upon salaries without us. By empowering the girls with more of a stake in the business they became the heart of Salvador's.

CHAPTER 13

WIND AT OUR BACKS

In 2008, Salvador's was trucking through its fourth year of operations in Kunming. Business continued to grow and throughout the city, people were talking about our homemade ice cream and coffees. Our menu continued to expand and covered a wide range of Mexican, Mediterranean and American foods. Most Kunming locals had little experience with international cuisine beyond pizza and burgers, but with ice cream as a kind of 'gateway drug,' local customers were soon munching on quesadillas, spaghetti Bolognese and teriyaki chicken salads.

Salvador's became a hip hangout for local college students during the day and for wealthier elite at night. The foreign population in Kunming grew rapidly those first few years so we had regulars from all over the world. The Salvador's family grew to include many of our customers and Salvador's became a kind of home away from home for many expats and Chinese alike.

Salvador's wasn't alone in the neighborhood. Though the Prague Café and French Café were in the area before us, there were even more who came after. Wenhua Xiang, the narrow alley connecting Yunnan University to Wenlin Street, was lined with an assortment of western cafés along with Chinese, Indian, Korean, Vietnamese and Japanese restaurants.

Our Chinese regulars covered a broad spectrum with varied ages, backgrounds and social status. The typical foreign customer, on the other hand, was most often a student or teacher from one of the nearby schools. Wenhua Xiang was the most common place in Kunming to see foreigners, which earned it the nickname, Foreigners' Street.

One day we had a visit from actor Edward Norton and magician David Blaine. They seated themselves upstairs at one of our larger tables. When we told the girls how internationally famous they were, the girls got too nervous to go up and take their order. Due to my years as a professional server back in Colorado, I stepped up to the job. But as soon as I approached the table I started having difficulty breathing. Being "star struck" always seemed like such a childish reaction to me, but there I was, in mid-order, when I started to hyperventilate. I asked them to please hold on for one minute and I made a dash for the office to catch my breath.

After a few minutes of embarrassing panic I returned to their table to finish taking their order. The food slowly made its way out to their table, but after about 15 minutes Mr. Norton came halfway down the spiral staircase, searched me out and said, "Hey man, did you forget my burrito?" From that day on, every time someone's order was forgotten, it's been called "getting Nortoned."

Next to Salvador's entrance was a solid-wood bar top paired with a removable stainless steel bar top that together could seat nine people. Expats in all parts of the world tend to cling to their beer and liquor as essential to the acculturation process of living abroad, and in Kunming it was no different.

When we introduced an extended happy hour from 4 to 8 PM, the bar stools filled up with regulars seeking cheap rum-cokes and gin-tonics on a daily basis. Because the bar ran along a major pedestrian thoroughfare, students, children, families and everyone else who walked by often stopped to take photos or just gawk at the seemingly alien beings occupying our bar stools. It was a useful advertisement that lured first time customers who were curious to see what Salvador's was all about.

As Salvador's became more popular, our staff increased to 16. About half of them had already worked with us for more than three years and this allowed them to take on even more of our responsibilities.

Almost all of the Salvador's girls came from just four villages in Lincang, and because of their relationships with each other, they were more or less self-governing. Not only did older employees train new girls to do their work in Salvador's, but they also counseled each other with issues at home – like relationship or health issues. They cared for each other at least as much as we cared for them. This of course brought about conflicts that would arise anywhere two girls lived and worked together for so long, let alone. But they handled these problems themselves and rarely brought them to work.

Our own partnership still had internal conflicts. I was always trying to spend more money to make more money, and Naoko was always trying to cut costs and save more money. We were like a small congress. I would propose something like a bill to remodel the kitchen and then Naoko would slash out the costs she saw as excessive, thus passing a slimmed down version of the original bill. It was a constant tug-of-war between us, but the end result was a good balance of saving and reinvesting.

After the first two years, we were able to pay back our initial investment and start making some real money. For the first time in years, we found ourselves with free time and extra cash in our pockets. Josh and I joined a basketball league, Naoko took over as accountant for Kunming's Japanese business society, and Kris toured the country as a late night music DJ. After four years of hard work, we were all starting to rediscover our lives outside of Salvador's.

It was about that time that I bought my new motorcycle. Toward the end of my first year in Dali, back in 2002, I had bought my first motorcycle. I'd never even ridden one before, but I planned a little solo trip to explore some of Yunnan's less-traveled back roads. I had no idea what to expect so I even strapped a machete to the side of the bike just in case I encountered dangerous situations. Everywhere I went, however, I found friendly people who always went out of their way to take care of me. They'd help me fix my bike for free, they'd have me over for lunch, and if it was late they'd do their best to get me drunk.

The motorcycle served as a vehicle for my first real introduction to rural China. On two wheels, with a four-stroke engine and off-road suspension, I was able to venture far from any city, and I fell in love with Yunnan's countryside.

Motorcycles are often the only easy way to connect many of Yunnan's villages to the outside world. Their hills are woven together with small dirt trails that are just wide enough to handle a horse or a motorcycle. Whether exploring interesting landscapes, ethnic minority villages or photogenic farming areas, the motorcycle offers access to remote places.

There are many parts of China where I've been so astounded by the beautiful countryside that I couldn't help but sing. I've made up my share of dirty songs ranging from promiscuity in a swimming pool to seductive Tibetan nomads. I would never repeat any of these songs to anyone, but at high speed out on the highway, I'd merrily belt them out at full volume with no one but myself to hear.

Yunnan's countryside is dotted with a diverse spectrum of villages. Some occupy high valleys surrounded by alpine forests while others sit in vast lowlands where sugarcane plantations stretch far and wide. Some villages contain only a few families deep in the mountains who tend small farms while others are packed with hundreds of families that together maintain large-scale agricultural businesses. Add to this an ethnic and cultural diversity that few places in the world can rival, and Yunnan is one of the most interesting places in Asia to travel. With a motorcycle, it is possible to spend a number of years exploring Yunnan's winding roads, terraced valleys and alpine terrain, yet still feel like there is more to see.

In late July 2008, one month before Beijing would be hosting China's first Olympics, Josh, Kris and I planned a trip in the Altai Mountains near China's borders with Russia and Mongolia. On August 1st, there was going to be a total solar eclipse centered along the mountain range. I scouted out a point on the map that appeared to be the best place to witness the rare event, and the three of us decided to ride out into the wilderness and watch from high in the mountains. By then we were all experienced riding motorcycles in China, but none of us had ever ridden so far off the beaten path.

We expected Xinjiang to be a bit different from Yunnan as it was a place that had far less cultural ties to the rest of China. The Altai Mountains in Xinjiang are home to thousands of Kazakhs who lead semi-nomadic lives. By horse and by motorcycle they lead their herds of goats up the valleys to high-mountain grasses during the summer after the snow melt. There they set up yurts that can sleep up to 20 people under the stretched leather and canvas. Their summers are spent weaving wool, churning butter and yogurt and shepherding in the mountain valleys. During the snowy winters, they hunker down to lower altitudes, seeking out the best lands for their animals' survival.

For two weeks we rode along small river valleys. Some nights we camped near hot springs or small rivers with the star-filled sky as our only shelter, but often Kazakh hospitality intervened and we were welcomed to stay in family yurts. At a hot springs nature reserve along the Mongolian border we met a local forest ranger named Bataar. He was a big man with an imposing presence and hands like a bear, but he spoke with a soft, mustachioed smile. He took us in and offered us his home and his food to use as our own.

Bataar had a summer wife at the hot springs and a winter wife down in the desert. His summer wife had two children by another man, but Bataar treated them as he would his own. One evening, the family welcomed us into their yurt and we snacked on meats and yogurt. After we shared a few warm beers with Bataar, the daughter turned down the lights, popped a tape cassette into a small, battery-powered boom box, and blasted 90s dance music. Her mother grabbed the flashlight and flickered it on and off like a strobe light. It was a homemade disco and the teenage daughter danced for us while Bataar, Josh and I cheered her on.

As the eclipse approached, we rode into another river valley where the road was more difficult but promised a better view of the solar event. We pitched our tents, bought some homemade yogurt and bread from nearby yurts, and watched as the moon passed directly in front of the sun.

Everything started to go dark and the insects and bats all suddenly awoke from their daytime slumber in a panic, thinking they had overslept. In a feeding frenzy, the larger flying insects started picking off the smaller flying insects as the bats hunted them both. The sky then turned black as night but for a faint, fiery blue ring in the sky. It was beautiful, and for a moment the world felt out of place. In the ecstasy of cosmic bewilderment, we watched as the halo of light dimly sparkled overhead.

At the end of it all, the moon revealed the sun again and the sky returned to normal.

We lived in China for experiences like this. For us, China was more than just a place where we had an opportunity to start a business. China was a place where we could hop on our motorcycles, point them in any direction, and ride into new adventures – and we rarely needed to worry about our safety. That's not to say that Chinese back country roads aren't full of dangerous obstacles, as dogs, tractors and even children seem to materialize out of nowhere. But never have I felt unwelcome among the local people. For the most part, no matter where you are in China, there will be those who go out of their way to welcome outsiders. Xinjiang was considered by many to be a volatile region, with ethnic uprisings and independence movements, but we never received anything but gracious hospitality.

Like Tibet, Xinjiang is not called a 'province' of China, but an 'autonomous region.' This is because the majority of people in Xinjiang, at least until very recently, have not been Han Chinese but Uighurs, an ethnic group of Turkish descent. Xinjiang had been virtually autonomous for decades under various rulers before the incursion of the People's Liberation Army in 1949, and many in Xinjiang resent the Han Chinese as occupiers and colonists today.

Less than five months before our motorcycle trip to Xinjiang, anti-Han Chinese riots in Tibet had resulted in hundreds of deaths and thousands of arrests; and while we were in Xinjiang, anti-Chinese sentiment in the region was near a tipping point. Leading up to the 2008 Olympics, a number of terrorist threats were made against Chinese authority. China was on the world stage, thanks to the Olympics, and independence factions in Xinjiang were hoping to take advantage of the press coverage, even by threatening violence.

When we returned to Xinjiang's capital, Urumqi, we settled into a small international hotel and clicked on the television news. We were shocked to learn that a terrorist had reportedly detonated two bombs on two different buses in Kunming only a few blocks from Salvador's. Two people had died in the blasts and more than a dozen were injured. The Turkestan Islamic Party, a faction in Xinjiang that sought independence from China, claimed responsibility for the blasts, but the investigation led to no arrests.

Violence like this was not totally unheard of in places like Tibet and Xinjiang, but in Kunming it was. Kunming was no terrorist target, but the country was changing, and perhaps Kunming was not quite the safe haven we had imagined it to be.

CHAPTER 14

AN UNEXPECTED GUEST

The weather was particularly nice for mid-winter in Kunming when Li Yan started his day. The sun was already shining bright when he rose from bed.

It was Christmas Eve and Salvador's was expecting a full house of 60 or so rather festive and intoxicated customers later in the evening. Li Yan had no interest in this and was only at Salvador's for breakfast and a hot coffee. For the rest of the day, he had much grander plans.

He arrived at Salvador's only minutes after it opened. He sat down at one of the corner tables on the first floor and ordered a waffle and a mocha with whipped cream. He was quiet and mostly kept to himself, but he knew that the day was no ordinary day.

That morning I awoke about an hour earlier than usual. I distinctly remember feeling like I'd slept deeper and better than I had in a long time. It was the kind of sleep where your body feels like a squeezed sponge, drained of all stress and anxiety. I was refreshed and took a look at the list of chores that needed to be done at Salvador's.

Frank, a familiar face at Salvador's, greeted me when I arrived. He was in town on leave from work to visit his mother over New Year's. Now a businessman in Hangzhou, Frank is originally from Kunming and usually showed up in Salvador's around the holidays. His black suit distinguished him from most of our typical customers, and he was always up for a casual chat. As he went back to typing at his computer I opened up my laptop on the communal Internet table in the middle of the restaurant's ground floor. Frank pulled out a cigarette and a waitress politely reminded him that it was Wednesday, and Wednesday was No Smoking Day, so he went outside for a cigarette before ordering his breakfast.

I started making measurements for how much closed-cell foam would be needed to repack the second-floor sofas as they started sagging from years of compaction from customer use. A group of three caffeinated Korean girls chatted noisily behind me as I punched numbers into the calculator.

An Australian friend came in with her two children and I put my work aside for a moment to chat with her. "I'm doing some last minute Christmas shopping," she told me. "You have any ideas where I can get some little gifts in the area?"

Kris and I had recently opened a small gift shop that sold Thai imports just around the corner so I told her that even though it was closed that day, I could let her in to see if there was anything she might want. The idea piqued her interest, so I left my computer on the table and we started down the street.

Meanwhile, Li Yan took one last bite of his waffle, picked up his small black shoulder bag and went into the bathroom. He locked the door and carefully unzipped his bag. Inside was an iron pipe that he had carefully packed with ammonium nitrate the day before along with a battery charge.

He attached the wires, set the timer, put the bomb back in his bag and zipped it closed. He washed his hands and dried them on the towel hanging under the glass sink. He turned the handle of the bathroom door, pulled it open and was only able to take one step before the bomb in his little black shoulder bag detonated prematurely, severing his lower body at the buttocks and launching him out of the bathroom face first to the feet of the café's shocked patrons.

My friend and I were only about 50 meters down the road when we heard the blast. We looked at each other and I said something like, "Wow, that was a big one." The road had been under construction for months, so loud noises were pretty common; but this thunderous sound was different. I turned around to see what had happened and saw a puff of smoke billowing out of Salvador's along with a few panicked customers. "Go, go!" my friend yelled as I ran to find out what had happened.

Running back into the restaurant took only a few seconds, but it felt like time had slowed, and nauseating panic radiated from deep in my gut. I assumed that our gas line had exploded and I feared the worst. I was already envisioning the demise of Salvador's. We might even go to prison for some sort of safety violation. I felt my life suddenly shift out of gear, stall and get stuck in neutral. "What if someone has been hurt?" I asked myself. I'd never be able to live with the guilt if we were somehow responsible for the injury of one of our customers or employees.

I ran through the smoke straight to the gas line and turned it off, but our gas line seemed to be intact and there was no fire. A piercing wail came from our workers in the kitchen and brought my attention to the remains of a body sprawled out on the floor only a few steps from my feet. Though I knew it was a human body, it seemed more like the mangled packaging that a body had once filled. It was a blobbish bag of bloodied flesh, with appendages twisted around it and a torso that had been ripped off at the buttocks.

Everything passed in frame-by-frame slow motion, and for a brief moment that felt like an eternity, I thought that the body was that of one of our workers. My initial instinct was that it was Xiao Hua, one of our workers who had come to Salvador's by way of a mutual friend. She was the tallest of all of our workers and the body was too big to be that of any of the other girls. She had worked at Salvador's for nearly two years and all of us had a close relationship with her. Like all of the girls, she was more family than employee. The moment of mourning penetrated deep into my psyche and repeated the tormenting words, "We've killed one of the girls."

I was frozen in time and space, although I wanted more than anything to escape. I wanted to teleport, to time travel, anything to get out. I wished we'd never opened Salvador's and that I'd never come to China in the first place. I wished we'd never put these girls in harm's way. It was our fault and we were irresponsible, contemptible, selfish people to have ever opened the business in the first place.

All of my goals and aspirations were suddenly meaningless and never again would I be able to pursue them. My life was over and it was now time to face my punishment, whatever it was that the world wished to dispense upon me.

I blinked, and time started moving forward again. My paralysis ended and I snapped back into action. The girls came running out of the kitchen, hurtling over the mangled body as they went past. One, two, three, four … they were all there. I'd passed the other three girls who were on shift near the entrance when I first scrambled in. That meant that all seven Salvador's girls were okay – at least okay enough not to be the body lying at my feet.

After turning off the gas line I ran toward the fuse box to switch everything off to avoid any sort of short that could start a fire. It was then that I noticed that there were hundreds of 100-yuan notes scattered all over the dining room tiles. The red-inked face of Mao Zedong printed on the money seemed to stare passively up at the ceiling. Amidst the cash, there was a black and red high-top basketball shoe. It had belonged to the body. The image of that shoe stamped itself indelibly in my memory.

I continued my dash to the electric box only to find that A Li had gotten there first. She assured me that all of our other customers had exited safely, and we hurriedly flipped off the remaining power switches. We then accompanied each other from behind the bar toward the door. As we passed the scattered money, A Li asked, "Should we pick it up?" I think we were both already in shock, and the thought of cleaning up the mess had strangely crossed my mind too. But reason got the better of us and we left the scene behind.

Seeing all seven faces of the Salvador's girls outside was a tremendous relief. They were all accounted for and were okay. Frank had been sitting only a couple of feet away from where the body lay, but he seemed unfazed by the event and calmly lit a cigarette. I was astounded by his indifference so I approached him to make sure he understood the gravity of the situation. His face went pale when I mentioned the body, which he had not noticed through the smoke.

It's a sad age we live in when one can so quickly recognize a suicide bombing has occurred, but it was the conclusion that I soon reached. My distorted world quickly began to rematerialize. After what had happened in the Bali bombing of 2002, and being that Christmas Eve is obviously significant for foreigners, I felt certain that we had been targeted by a man, or maybe even a group, with malicious intent. It was an oddly reassuring idea, because it meant that the explosion was not our fault.

Frank began to panic as everything sank in. He was extremely lucky to be alive. Had the bomb exploded just a few seconds later, or had the bomber turned around to check himself out in the mirror, Frank would have been seriously injured – or worse.

I called Kris, who was still home, and while sobbing into the phone I said something like, "Our life as we know it is over. Come over now. There's been an explosion." I can't imagine the irreparable damage that this call could have done to Kris. I spoke far too bluntly, not considering how terrifying such a phone call might be for him. It was unfair not to have given him a clearer explanation so I called him right back and said, "We are all okay, but someone blew themselves up right next to the kitchen."

"I'll be right there," he said calmly. Sure enough, before the ambulance arrived, Kris came running up to us. We were huddled together next to the entrance. My adrenaline-fueled focus dissipated, and now my emotions took over. The reality of the moment fell heavy upon me. As the nine of us sobbed in one big group hug, I couldn't help but fear the future. We had no idea what now lay ahead for our restaurant, for our girls and for our lives in China. Nothing seemed certain anymore.

When the ambulance arrived, we realized we'd been surrounded by a horde of onlookers. More than a hundred people gazed at us as if watching a movie, whispering to each other about what they thought would happen next. I approached one of the men in uniform and told him that they needed to inform all the restaurants in the neighborhood to be on the lookout. It being Christmas Eve, I assumed we were the target of some sort of anti-foreign attack. Recalling the money scattered on the floor, it seemed quite plausible that there was some sort of organization involved, and that other restaurants with foreigners might be at risk. The officer gave me a confused look. It seemed that everyone still thought that this was an accident for which we were responsible.

Qin Hui, our crusader in action, arrived a few minutes later. After offering the girls some placating words of consolation, he took over as our liaison with the police. The medics were tending to the body inside the restaurant and I suddenly had the guilty feeling that maybe I should have checked for a pulse or performed a basic assessment of the 'victim's' vitals. Maybe I could have helped. But it was too late for me to do anything – I could see the medics inside now dragging the body toward the front door. I jumped down off the front patio and told the girls to look away. With ages from 17 to 25, the girls had already witnessed too much carnage that day and I didn't want them to see any more. They all did as I asked, but Qin Hui gagged twice as he looked upon the twisted and contorted body that had once been living.

The medics pulled Kris and me aside after they placed the body in the ambulance. They said that we needed to come to the back of the vehicle to identify the body. We pleaded with them that it was unnecessary and that we had no connection to the bomber, but the police were suspicious that perhaps it was a former employee or a jealous boyfriend, so we did as they asked.

We tentatively approached the back of the ambulance to view the perpetrator. The body's face looked strangely passive and free of pain. His body was deflating like a mound of risen bread dough after being tossed onto a baking sheet. Although he appeared to be dead, his eyes still held a spark of life. He seemed to be looking at me. I looked into his eyes and it almost felt as if he was trying to say something.

The police insisted that either Kris or I needed to accompany the body to the hospital. My objections fell upon disinterested ears. Kris stepped in and said that he would go, and that I should stay with the girls. It was a sacrifice for which I was very grateful. He left with the police, who followed the ambulance to the hospital. The girls and I, along with Frank and the three Korean girls, were led down the street to the police station.

Along the way, I managed to my phone my father. I told him, "Dad, there's been a bombing at Salvador's and I can't really talk right now, but we're all okay." The call must have come as quite a shock, but unfortunately I was unable to offer a more thorough explanation as the police insisted I put my cell phone away.

As we approached the police station, I noticed a small chunk of red meat on top of the suitcase that Frank wheeled behind him. It was a piece of the bomber's pink flesh and I suddenly felt woozy. When I told Frank, he swatted it off in a fit of disgust.

Every time the girls tried talking with each other, the police got in our face and angrily told us we were not permitted to speak. This infuriated me, and I asked why we were being treated like suspects instead of victims. They insisted that we all remain silent until after investigators had time to interview each of us separately. During my interview I broke into tears numerous times. For the first hour after the bombing, my world seemed to disintegrate and reassemble itself every few minutes. Personal tragedy had reached me only a few times in my life, with the death of friends or family, but never had anything thrown me into such shock. It was difficult to piece together what was real and what was not.

At times I wondered if maybe the shock had made me forget what had actually happened. Maybe the stress of the situation had caused my mind to shift into some sort of self-defense mechanism. Maybe Xiao Hua, the girl I initially thought had died, was actually dead and things were worse than I was willing to acknowledge. It was hard to get a fix on reality, and the questions from the detective did little to help me get my story straight.

The thought of Kris at the hospital with the bomber felt so wrong. I repeatedly asked the detective if he could find out where Kris was and if he was okay, but, in keeping with procedure, he could give me no information. Luckily, Qin Hui was given the freedom to float between rooms, and he assured me that all of the girls and Kris were fine.

After a few more hours of interviews, Kris was brought back to the police station and it was officially announced that we were at no fault for the explosion. With this announcement, the police eased off of the girls and me and let us finally talk and cry together. Other than some ringing in the ears, they were all okay. I was able to give Xiao Hua a big hug and I finally found my senses again.

Kris had spent most of the day at the hospital in the room next to the bomber. It was horrifying to hear that the bomber had still been alive when I looked into his eyes in the ambulance. In fact he lived another two hours. Kris was in the next room when the legless, dying man admitted to bombing the two buses the previous August. Kris did not hear the confession but overheard the doctors say that he had confessed. The police even borrowed Kris' phone to record the bomber's last moments and supposed confession – a recording that had already been erased when they returned the phone.

It was an eerie feeling to have looked into the eyes of a man who had come so close to taking the lives of people I cared for. Learning that he had still been breathing when we looked into each other's eyes in the back of the ambulance made the moment that much more intense. I hoped that for him at least, the moment offered some sort of closure.

After about nine hours, all the reports had been filed and we were finally allowed to leave the police station. The girls seemed to be handling everything as well as could be expected and just wanted to go home and rest. Kris and I went to my place, where Aling had prepared dinner for us. We'd barely eaten anything all day, but I was hardly hungry. Entering the door of our apartment I was greeted by friends Wang Hu and Zhang Yunbin. I barely got the words "*da-ge*," meaning "brother," out before I started sobbing like I hadn't cried since childhood.

Josh and Naoko were then back in America visiting family, but that night they were able to reach me by phone. I tried my best to keep them from panicking and stressed the fact that everyone was okay, but I could scarcely manage a complete sentence without sobbing. They promised to return as soon as they could, but I had no idea what they would be coming back to.

After this conversation the tears continued to flow. I spent most of the night in bouts of tears, trying not to think about what could have happened. Trying not to think about how close the girls had been to the detonation of an ammonium nitrate pipe bomb. Trying not to think about what could have happened if the bomb had gone off only five seconds later. And trying not to think about the image of what I thought was Xiao Hua's body splayed out on the floor.

I remembered my shark encounter in Thailand 10 years earlier, when I had spent the night tossing and turning in my tent thinking about what might have been if my luck had gone a little differently. It was then too that I turned to thoughts about my place in the world and how my decisions affect it. Had my universe actually split into two when the bomb went off? Was I now living in a universe where only the bomber had died, while an alternate version of me in a parallel universe was dealing with the death of one of our employees? In another universe, had I been eaten by sharks?

Everything seemed fragile, as if every single decision I'd ever made in my life had fractured my entire world and that, with each decision, it might have run a different course. And I felt sorry for myself – sorry for the other me, who was now coping with the death of Xiao Hua.

My thoughts were irrational but tortuously inescapable. For the next few days, I learned that my mind was not necessarily at my command. My imagination followed its own trajectory. I was stuck in the moment when I thought I saw Xiao Hua's body on the floor. I was in an alternate reality of what might have happened and it made me feel sick, angry and powerless. I was tortured by the false reality, but I could find some solace in the fact that everyone was actually okay – at least everyone that I cared about.

CHAPTER 15

DAMAGE CONTROL

I had cried myself to sleep and woke up throughout the night with disturbing dreams. I still felt like we'd lost everything, that our lives in China had come to an end and that Salvador's would never again open its doors. I was feeling powerless and all that I had to look forward to that day was a bloody mess around Table Five.

The morning after the bombing, Chinese news reports varied wildly. One said that there was no bomb, and that a gas delivery man had dropped a canister which exploded and killed one of our customers. Another said that our gas line had ignited, killing one of our workers. Still more devised conspiracies about terrorism and cover-ups. It was as if the worst fears of my alternate realities were being broadcast to the world.

It was Christmas and most reporters in the Western world were on vacation. So a story that usually would have made international headlines never really made any news. It wasn't that I wanted to make news, but most people in Kunming awoke that day believing that we were responsible for an accident that had killed someone, and the idea that fake news was spreading made me want to at least straighten out the story.

Chris Horton, a close friend who did all he could to help us the day of the explosion, ran an English news website about Kunming called Go Kunming. In an effort to address the problem of misinformation, he let me post the following explanation on the site.

At a press conference on Saturday, the police tied the bomber of Salvador's to the bomber of the public buses back in July. There was DNA evidence that links both crimes, and bomb materials were found at the home of the suspect that are the same as the bombs used on the buses and our cafe. The suspect had served several years in prison for an assault-related crime.

For most expats who have lived in China for some time, it's very easy to be skeptical of the media, and this report seems so convenient to solve two crimes in one shot. But from our experiences with this investigation, we both feel very confident in Saturday's report. In addition, we thought you'd all like to know that the police have treated us quite well and have been extremely professional with the handling of the investigation.

It was also revealed that the bomb was in the bathroom and appears to have exploded prematurely. The night of the 24th is perhaps the busiest night of the year for cafes in the neighborhood, and I can only assume that the bomber had higher aspirations than the outcome. We are lucky in so many ways, it's really quite difficult to talk about.

For now, our greatest concern is the mental and physical health of our workers. We have been spending time together discussing the event and making sure that everything gets talked through. Everyone is in much better spirits now, and we hope to move on. The future of our business is at present uncertain, but you have not heard the last of Salvador's.

Thank you for all of your kind words and support.

What irritated me the most the day after the bombing was that everyone talked about it as an accident. What was an accident exactly? It was true that the bomber *accidentally* detonated the bomb, *accidentally* exploding himself into pieces all over our restaurant. But the fact was that he walked into Salvador's that day with "killing people" on his to-do list, so classifying his act as an accident seemed disingenuous. Though he may have botched his plans by triggering the bomb prematurely, it was no accident that he was carrying a live bomb in his little black shoulder bag. If that day he had triggered his bomb as planned, he would have been called a terrorist. Instead, his act only made news as an accident. To me, this made the bomber seem like the victim.

Media reports revealed that Li Yan had recently served a five-year stint in prison for robbery and assault. During his time in prison he worked as an electrician, and it was believed that this experience may have helped him learn to make bombs. Ammonium nitrate, bomb-casing materials and a homemade gun were found at his residence, and there was enough evidence to identify him as the bus bomber from the previous summer. As more evidence was released, it seemed increasingly unlikely that Salvador's was the intended target and more probable that he had only used our bathroom in order to piece together a bomb to detonate on another bus.

Kris and I met the next day to discuss what to do about the girls. Whether or not we reopened, there was no reason to keep them in Kunming at a time when they'd prefer to return to their families. We all had witnessed far too much violence and mayhem so we were worried about any psychological trauma they may have suffered. Trauma counseling is kind of a foreign idea in China, so we had to do our best on our own.

We called all of the girls over to my apartment around lunch time. We sat out on the patio under the blue sky and talked. We relived the experience, we talked about what the body looked like, we talked about how lucky we were, we talked about the future, we cried, we hugged and we cried some more. It was cathartic for everyone.

One of the girls, Yaya, had only just started working with us a month earlier when she came to Kunming with us from Ali's wedding. She was young, she was shy, and every time I looked at her, I felt horribly guilty about her leaving her peaceful mountain village only to come to the city to witness such carnage. But with all of them there together – safe and healthy – I too was comforted.

We had an amazing crew of young women who had left their families and their homes behind to try to make it in the city. Through all that had happened that day, they took care of each other with dignity and compassion. I gained extra respect for them and promised myself never to undervalue their hard work and loyalty.

During those first two days after the bombing, we were fortunate to have a number of friends around to support us. Moe, a friend from Myanmar who had lived in Dali about the same time as I had, was one of the first to check up on us. He ran a restaurant in a bar in town and invited all of us to spend the next day on the rooftop for a lunch buffet. He prepared a massive feast of Burmese and Chinese food that instantly had us talking about things other than the bombing. We ate, played foosball and kicked the *jianzi* – a kind of feathered hacky sack. Most importantly, we laughed. It was the greatest gift Moe could give. He brought laughter to all of us when there had been only fear and sorrow.

All 18 girls boarded buses for their respective villages the next day and Kris and I were left to figure things out. The police still wouldn't let us back into the restaurant so we couldn't even clean up the mess. We consulted with a lawyer who told us that any attempt to appeal for monetary compensation for the damage done to Salvador's would be futile. We didn't even know if we could ever reopen. Trapped in limbo, we were overwhelmed with apprehension about what to do next.

China had been my home for nearly eight years. Living in China as a foreigner, one is always an outsider, someone who lives on the fringe of society. But I had never felt the kind of isolation that I did those first two days after the bombing.

When I finally mustered the courage to walk past the storefront, I saw a sign taped to the door that read, "We support you!" and "加油," a Chinese phrase meant to cheer us on. Many others had added their own encouragements in both Chinese and English. It was a small gesture, but it showed that the community was behind us and that maybe there was a way forward, one in which Salvador's would live on.

CHAPTER 16

BLADE TO THE CHICKEN'S THROAT

A spiritual medium met A Li at her family's mountaintop home. He punctured the neck of a chicken with a small blade and collected its blood in a porcelain bowl. A Li watched the chicken cling to life with the very last of its strength before finally giving in.

It was a sacrifice for the *jiaohun*, or "spirit calling ceremony." In village life, it is believed that mental traumas chase away the spirit. The spirit loses its way, roaming aimlessly, and leaves the body susceptible to sickness. The medium said that the bombing had created a schism between A Li's physical self and her spirit. The ceremony was the only way to make her whole again.

Since the bombing, A Li hadn't been able to get much sleep, and when she did manage to get any, it was clouded with nightmares. She was afraid of the dark, haunted by gruesome and frightening visions. When she returned to her parents' home from Kunming they immediately insisted that she see the village medium, a kind of shaman who could help her find her lost spirit.

The medium burned incense and waved it about the room to rid the space of any lingering harmful spirits. He then placed bowls of rice next to the sacrificed chicken and began pacing back and forth, working himself into a trance. His eyed fluttered and his movements became odd and erratic.

Suddenly he cried out in a deep guttural voice, "A Li! A Li! Let A Li's spirit return and be cleansed! Return, A Li! Return!" He repeated this over and over in a plea to the spirit realm to guide A Li's spirit back to her and heal the scars of her trauma. Again he cried out, louder this time, "Return, A Li! Return, A Li! Return, A Li!"

"I am here!" A Li yelled. "I have returned!" It was what her parents had told her to say in response to the medium's performance, but she had not expected to be so exhilarated by it. The medium tied a red string around her left bicep, once again bonding her spirit with her body. Then together they ate the offerings.

"The whole thing had me feeling rather skeptical," A Li later told me. "It was strange and kind of stupid, but I have to say I slept better that night than I had since the bombing. My dreams had been so horrible, but after the ceremony everything was so much better."

Most of the girls working the day of the bombing went through similar ceremonies and experienced similar results. They slept better and they were able to get rid of the terrible visions that haunted them. In the days after the bombing I found myself wondering how my spirit would find its way back to me.

*   *   *

Six days after the explosion the police finally finished their investigation and let us back into the restaurant. It was exactly the same as we had left it. A long wide smear of dried blood greeted Kris and me at the entrance. It led all the way to the back of the restaurant, from where the medics had dragged the body. There was a large pool of dried blood where the bomber landed after he was launched from the bathroom. It was dried and cracked, peeling up around the edges from the floor.

The smell of the blast still lingered, like the smoke from the cap guns I played with when I was young. Glass from the exploded bathroom door was everywhere and a few shards of metal from the bomb casing were embedded in the wall near where Frank had been sitting – a reminder of just how lucky he was.

The sight of the blood didn't really disturb me. I'd seen it already and it wasn't nearly as shocking as when the body was there. Initially, we thought we could manage to clean up the whole mess on our own – that was until we saw globs of human fat and tissue from the blast on the walls, the tables and even on the front windows at the other end of the restaurant. There was no way we could stomach doing the work ourselves, so we hired a cleaning crew. They too hesitated when they saw what they were getting into, but they took the job after we offered them twice the normal rate.

That first week, I felt very strongly that reopening would be a mistake. Putting our girls and ourselves in harm's way again was out of the question, and for me, opening again was asking for trouble. It seemed that the sensible solution would be to sell everything and hope to walk away with enough money to start something new.

Josh and Naoko returned a few days later. It was so good to see them. I think that Kris and I were still in shock, so their arrival helped refocus our thoughts. With them back, a hint of normalcy returned and it suddenly seemed that perhaps there was a way forward. They were not ready to give up, and I realized that neither was I. Together again, the four of us decided to work toward reopening.

Josh started things off with a few wild swings of the hammer. First he smashed the ceiling supports. Then he took a swing into the ceiling's plywood, where the hammer stuck in deep. He did a little dance of destruction, as Josh enjoyed smashing things. We all laughed, and soon joined in the smashing.

We decided to scrap everything, totally gutting the place, so we could start over from scratch. We ripped out the second floor, knocked down the walls and finally got rid of the ugly pink floor tiles that had been left over from the Korean restaurant.

At one point, as Josh and I carried a table out of the restaurant to put into storage, I could feel a strange greasiness on my palms and fingers. A revolting feeling mounted in my belly. The cleaning crew apparently didn't do as thorough a job as we had hoped. Kris was reaching the same conclusion as he handled other furniture inside. He chased after us panicked. His eyes were tearing and his face was drained of color.

"It's, it's …" Kris said while dry-heaving. "Put it down!" He gagged again. "It's fat! It's human fat!"

Josh and I had already realized this, but we had decided to keep on going anyway. Our hands were already covered in it and there was no sense in stopping. Kris looked on in dismay, still choking back the urge to vomit.

We got rid of everything, and soon Salvador's was as bare as could be. It looked so small when empty – it was hard to imagine that just two weeks earlier it had been a restaurant packed full of customers. Revolting mess that it was, it was refreshing to get it cleaned up, like a spring cleaning taken to the extreme. Salvador's was again a blank sheet of paper, and we had the opportunity for a rewrite.

We rethought the layout to make more seating available, said goodbye to the spiral staircase and took special pleasure in watching the concrete workers smash up the remaining pink tiles. The Koreans who had originally remodeled the space had built the second floor with wooden beams. There had been times when we wondered about the safety of the structure, as the supports bent and creaked from the weight of customers above. Now we had a chance to rebuild it with a solid steel frame.

The four of us went through a lot of the same issues as the first time. Figuring out paint colors, lighting and spacing brought back old arguments. But this time we were bonded with a new vision of our future together and a solid determination to right the wrong that the bomber had brought upon us.

Throughout the difficult month of reconstruction, we gained a new respect for each other. In the larger picture of what Salvador's was, our small differences and disagreements seemed trivial and petty. Once the initial shock of the bombing wore off, we weren't going to quit and we wouldn't use the bombing as an excuse. Rather, the bombing only made us more determined. Salvador's would not be a casualty, and we would not let the bomber's deranged and hateful act destroy what we had built.

After four weeks, all but one of our 18 girls came back from their villages to work with us again. I'm not so sure I would have done the same in their positions, but we were very happy to see them. They seemed to return with a renewed appreciation for the business we had built together. They reorganized the kitchen and prepared the restaurant for opening.

I was admittedly still a little uneasy. There was no guarantee that we wouldn't be attacked again. Maybe the bomber was part of some larger movement. Maybe we *had* been the intended target, and next time someone else would get the job done right. And wouldn't our customers be fearful? Why would anyone want to sip on a latte or buy ice cream for their children at a restaurant that had been bombed?

It was an emotional moment when we opened the big glass door again. Naoko could no longer hold back her tears and we all embraced. Everyone we knew in Kunming showed up, and so did many who we didn't know. The place was packed. Salvador's had survived, and the night turned out to be the busiest nights we'd had in four and a half years since opening in Kunming.

CHAPTER 17

HAUNTED BY GHOSTS

It was the same every night.

"Here it comes," I'd think to myself. First the earth would rumble. Then the walls would begin to crumble and I would know that my end had come.

I didn't trust the construction of Kunming's towering apartments. The city had grown too fast. Contractors had cut corners to save on costs and used shoddy materials and I knew that once the earthquake came, the buildings would quickly disintegrate and turn to rubble.

For the first year after the bombing, this happened at least three times each night. I'd wake up knowing that the earthquake was just about to happen. I could feel the pent-up energy far below me in the earth's mantle ready to be released. It felt as if it would come any second.

It was all in my head, of course, but some nights I really felt as if I could hear the sounds of fracturing concrete. I imagined Aling and me stumbling through the rumbling apartment and losing awareness of whether or not the floor even existed. When the concrete foundation could finally take no more, we would experience a brief moment of weightlessness. I would gasp for air, but none would come. My stomach would plunge with the nauseating feeling of free-fall as our seven-story apartment building collapsed. Bricks, mortar and twisted metal would crash all around. And then, after what seemed like an eternity, I would finally hit the ground, gravity releasing its might upon me. The rest of the building would follow soon after, and with a brief wince of pain everything would go dark.

I tortured myself with these dark visions. None of it was real, but I'd awaken each time, sure that it was. The anxiety would send my blood pressure up and soon my body would actually tremble, although it was from the racing pulses of the blood in my veins, not an earthquake.

I lived in an apartment only about a half-block from Salvador's. Every time I'd hear any noise at home I'd have to call the girls just to make sure nothing was wrong. I did it so many times that they began to worry about me, so I started pretending I was calling about scheduling or something else managerial. Once, when I thought I'd heard a loud crash and called, no one answered. I ran as fast as I could to the restaurant only to find that the ringer had been turned off by accident.

Even the ringer on my mobile phone took on a sinister role. Every time someone called, I assumed there was tragic news. That first note from my ringer stirred such an immediate anxiety attack that I had to change my ring tone just about every week. I was in a constant state of panic and when left to my own imagination, I'd often find myself living in an alternate reality where we had not been so lucky – one in which we had lost Xiao Hua.

The daydreams made me feel foolish and I was disappointed in myself for letting them take hold. Every day, thousands of people throughout the world suffered far more serious personal tragedies. I could never claim to know the suffering of someone who had that day lost a child in a car accident or had witnessed the devastation war had brought to their town. It seemed cowardly to wallow in self-pity or claim any of the same despair as those who experienced far worse than we had.

The reality was, considering all of the madness of the bombing, nothing catastrophic actually happened to Salvador's. We had been extremely lucky. Business was good and everyone was healthy. We suffered a temporary financial burden with the costs of remodeling, but as importantly, a murderer was off Kunming's streets without having caused any more casualties.

Still I couldn't make my fears go away. If like A Li, my problem was that my spirit was aimlessly wandering, severed from my physical self, I figured all I could do was to try to find it.

CHAPTER 18

COUNTRY LESSONS

Josh fumbled with the stick shift and appeared unable to change gears. "We just lost the clutch," he said with a desperate sigh.

"Shut up, dude," I said, hoping he was joking. "Don't mess with me."

"I wish I was, man, but we're stuck."

It couldn't have happened at a worse time. We had driven more than 13 hours over two days before reaching the high valley slope along the Lancang River, what further downstream in Laos is called the Mekong River. We had spent the last hour driving down a twisting dirt road, a road that would have been inaccessible by most cars. The rainy season had left deep ruts and some parts had been washed out altogether.

We were driving a 4-wheel-drive vehicle, so we were confident in our ability to navigate the terrain, but without a clutch there was no way we were going to get the car turned around and back up the rocky slope we had just descended. We were far from any mechanic, and you can't just call up AAA in China's countryside. Josh shut off the engine and we locked up the car to walk into the nearby village to look for help.

This wasn't just any village. It was Bangdong, the same village that Mengjuan had left at 14 years old to start a new life in Dali. Mengjuan initially introduced a number of cousins and friends from the village to Salvador's, so Bangdong, along with other nearby villages, was home to nearly half of the Salvador's staff.

We'd come to Bangdong with the hope of meeting our workers' parents. Salvador's employed 18 girls, 17 of which were from villages in Lincang

Prefecture. Josh and I planned to find each one of their homes and meet their families. We wanted to talk about the work their daughters were doing at Salvador's and offer them a group photo of our business. In turn we hoped to learn a bit about their lives in the village. The broken clutch threatened to cut our trip short.

It was late spring, and all around the valley, women and men worked diligently picking glossy tea leaves in the well-trimmed groves. They wore cone-shaped hats made of woven straw and bamboo to keep the hot sun off their faces and necks. While they worked, other farmers planted orderly rows of rice in shallow pools of water or plowed corn fields for a new seeding. The air was fragrant with the aromas of new foliage and soured by the stench of freshly turned manure. The skies above were clear and blue, but a dense fog blanketed the deep valley below us.

Neither of us had been to Bangdong before. We had no idea where to start looking for our workers' homes. We followed a dirt road that ran along a hilly ridge lined with terraced tea fields. The village was spread out along a steep slope and I started to understand why none of our girls ever learned to ride a bicycle. Even an experienced mountain biker would find the terrain challenging. The hills were steep, but the local farmers had still managed to transform every accessible piece of arable land into productive fields – an incredible feat considering that it was all done over many generations and without machinery.

We were greeted on the road by the curious grins of two old women carrying bamboo baskets filled with fresh tea leaves on their backs. They'd taken a break from the hot sun to find shade in a small bamboo grove. When we mentioned the girls' names they didn't seem to know them, but when we said their fathers' names the older woman lifted her crooked index finger and pointed down the hill.

A narrow path led to a wider road that had been cobbled with round river stones. This opened up into a larger square lined with old wooden homes. A group of women were carefully sorting their tea leaves before placing them on straw mats to dry in the sun. This filled the air with a strong but pleasant floral aroma. The tea sorters cast us a brief suspicious glance, then turned away to continue their work. A small dog chased a chicken up a nearby citrus tree. The chicken tried to fly to escape, but it failed and bounced when it hit the ground. Again the dog started up the chase.

We approached a small village shop selling beer, candy and cigarettes. I was about to ask the shop owner about one of the girls' families when we noticed a short skinny Chinese man with dreadlocks. This was not the typical style in the countryside, so he looked nearly as out of place as we did.

When he noticed us coming his way, he did an instant double-take. "Josh? Colin?" For a second or two, he didn't know what else to say. It was too unexpected an encounter to make any sense to him. We knew who he was, but we too were slow to accept it as reality.

"Zhuhong?" I finally said. It was the same kid that I knew from nearly seven years earlier as a little joint-smoking punk who had worked for the Bird Bar. "What the hell are you doing here?" I asked.

"This is my home, *man*." He spoke in Chinese, but emphasized "man" in English. "I think the better question is, what the hell are you two doing here?"

We shook hands and described our troubles with the 4x4. We had borrowed it from Wang Hu and were a bit anxious about how we could possibly get the car back up to the main road, so with Zhuhong there, the situation no longer felt so desperate.

Like Mengjuan, Zhuhong had grown up in Bangdong and moved to Dali to seek a new life. Unlike Mengjuan, however, Zhuhong's father had sent him to Dali to keep him out of prison.

"When I was 14 years old," Zhuhong told me, "I loved to fight. I'd go village to village fighting whoever I could. The roads were so bad back then that even the police could never catch up to me. My parents and sister would stay up late each night hoping I'd come home alive."

Zhuhong was short and scrawny but had a reputation as a ferocious fighter. Eventually, he used his talents to gain employment from local mafia leaders who hired him to collect protection money from brothels in nearby towns. He'd work long nights, going brothel to brothel collecting the cash. "If they refused to pay," he said, "I'd beat them badly."

One time, when a brothel owner refused payment and put up a fight, Zhuhong grabbed a sword and slashed the man on his neck and arms. The man nearly died, and this time the police finally caught up with Zhuhong. "I would have spent five years at a labor camp if my father hadn't paid off the officials with 30,000 Renminbi" (about $3,600 at the time). But getting his son out of prison wasn't enough. His father wanted him to find a way out of his violent lifestyle for good, so Zhuhong packed up and moved to Dali.

I met Zhuhong on my first day in Dali – the same day that I met Kris and Rongjie. Zhuhong worked for Rongjie at the Bird Bar and was notorious for getting into fights. Though I never saw that side of him, Josh had once seen him take part in the beating of a drunk foreigner at the bar. By the time I made it to Dali, the bohemian lifestyle of the small town had already rubbed off on him. He liked to smoke hand-rolled hashish, listen to reggae and shoot pool. Never did I see his violent side.

Zhuhong worked at the Bird Bar for about two years. For the next 10 years, he wandered to different parts of the province, and even farther, to Beijing and Shanghai. I'd see him every two years or so, but I had certainly not expected to run into him in Bangdong. It was an amazing coincidence and a fortuitous one.

He showed us around the village and introduced us to the families of our workers, many of whom Zhuhong had grown up with. He told us not to worry about the 4x4 as he'd figure something out the next day. So even though we were stranded, we were right where we wanted to be.

For me, China's countryside represented the kind of lifestyle I'd always idealized. It was a place where there were no concerns about traffic and pollution – where peoples' lives revolved around agriculture and family. The girls had come to Kunming for exactly opposite reasons. For them it was the city that held hope for their success. Oddly, it seemed that they sought a lifestyle that I had left behind, while I sought a lifestyle that they left behind.

Zhuhong took us to Pingdi's home first. Pingdi had started with us back when we still had Salvador's in Dali, and had continued to work with us for the next six years. She was not working the day of the Christmas Eve explosion at Salvador's, but she had rushed over when she heard the news. By the time she got there, we'd all been taken to the police station. There were still about a hundred onlookers at the scene, and they told her that one of the employees had died in a gas explosion. "My legs turned into noodles when I heard that," she said. "I nearly lost consciousness at the thought."

At just under 140 centimeters, Pingdi was shorter than everyone else at Salvador's. When you're short in China, it can be difficult to find work, but Pingdi never let that slow her down. She was one of the most tenacious workers we ever had and often squinted in a stubborn effort to avoid wearing glasses. Sharp-witted and energetic, she was never one to keep quiet about problems she noticed in the restaurant. We all considered Pingdi to be a very close friend, and we were excited when Zhuhong offered to introduce us to her family.

Zhuhong led us up steep muddy steps. A large growling dog with white and brown spots made us hesitate before Pingdi's mother called the dog back. Towering bamboo arched over the entryway, which made for a cool approach on an otherwise hot day. Pingdi's mother waved us over to a small table above the dirt courtyard. Next to this was a large stable that housed 10 cows that all wore clanging bells. A small orchestra rang through the valley each time Pingdi's mother threw feed into the cowshed.

A shy smile stretched across her face as she poured us tea. "Please don't go to any trouble on our account," we insisted as she scrambled to prepare food for us. Zhuhong knew Pingdi's mother well. In fact, as a youth he was originally selected to marry Pingdi's older sister. When they got older, the marriage never materialized, but the families still remained close. Zhuhong repeated our plea that we had just eaten and not to trouble to make anything. "They just really wanted to meet you," he said over and over.

Pingdi's mother was at least as short as her daughter. She couldn't have been older than 45, but she had a slightly hunched back and walked with a limp. Decades of picking tea in the hot sun had given her dark face deep wrinkles.

Pingdi's father showed up five minutes later with an ear-to-ear smile that belied how nervous he was to be around foreigners for the first time. Pingdi had been sending money home to her parents from the very first month she started working at Salvador's, so for us to show up at their house was awkward and disarming. We talked about how much Pingdi had learned at Salvador's and how skilled she was as a kitchen manager. They digested the compliments uneasily, as if they'd never thought of their daughter in that way. After a brief and uncomfortable silence, her father invited us to join him for a shot of homemade corn liquor. He breathed deeply, relishing the burn of the strong alcohol, then picked up a long walking stick, tied his shoes tight, smiled and waved goodbye before leading his 10 cows down the muddy slope.

"He's taking them out to pasture," Zhuhong told us. "He won't be back for eight hours or so as the pasture is about two kilometers away." He had to do that every single day. Skipping a day meant risking the health of the cattle, each valued at over 10,000 yuan ($1,600). His wife also got back to work breaking kernels of corn off the cob to dry them in the sun on the concrete patio overlooking the valley.

The sun was getting brutally hot as Zhuhong led us to the other families' homes. He also showed us where the old village school had been the makeshift four-person carousel on which he had played as a youth. A number of children chased each other around the small ride. The youngest ones wore the pants with open bottoms that young Chinese children often wear. When they squat to go to the bathroom, they avoid the need for diapers, leaving their refuse in the tall grass.

After a short hike up the hill, we arrived at Zhuhong's home. It was built in the typical local fashion – framed with rough logs and walled with mud brick. Two large black pigs feverishly slurped up a sloppy gruel made from corn and leftovers. A small flock of chickens pecked at rice and corn kernels thrown about the small concrete courtyard. Tata, the family's small black dog, jumped excitedly about us. From time to time he displayed his command of the household by chasing off a stray chicken.

Zhuhong's mother cornered one chicken with beautiful golden plumage spotted with white and black. She grabbed it by its feet, held it upside down and quickly punctured its throat with a blade. The chicken struggled for a few moments before the blood stopped flowing. The other chickens seemed to pay little attention. She then submerged the body in warm water for a minute before expertly plucking off all of its feathers and preparing it for dinner.

Zhuhong led us up to his room, a small addition that he had built a year earlier. We sat on a patio that overlooked the entire village and the expansive valley below. Dense fog was forming near the river while the sky took on the deep blue of a cloudless sunset. Zhuhong poured us warm tea made from leaves he had helped his mother pick and process that day. Then he tied his long dreadlocks behind his head and poured us each a shot of home-distilled liquor.

"What brought you back to Bangdong?" I asked.

His smile softened and I could tell he'd been asking himself the same question. In a sentimental voice he replied, "I feel like I've been wandering, lost, for the past 14 years." He swatted an annoying fly from his bare shoulder. "I felt it was time to come home. There's been something missing in my life, and I think I might find it here."

The people of Bangdong, like millions of other villagers in China, had watched for two decades as townships and cities modernized while little had changed in their villages. They continued to live the same as they always had with little outside help. However, those of the younger generation were increasingly drawn to the cities and parents were left on their own.

Zhuhong hoped to change this and to encourage his own brand of village development. He just wasn't sure where to start. Schools were underfunded and lacked the proper supplies and equipment. Health care was a mess – village-level doctors received little to no training and quality treatment elsewhere was often unaffordable. The price of tea had plummeted and income levels in Bangdong were often less than one dollar per day – not even enough to afford motorcycle fuel.

Village families in many parts of China live near subsistence level. They grow their own grains, vegetables and fruits, they raise their own animals, and they do all they can to save up a little money for their families. It is rarely sufficient however, so many families invest everything to send a child to the city in search of higher wages.

The girls working at Salvador's all came from similar situations. For them, leaving their families to work for us was an opportunity to increase the families' incomes. Some of our girls were the first of their generation to leave their village. Other neighboring families soon asked if their daughters could also work for us. Eventually, as many as 10 families from one small village could say that they had a daughter working in Kunming at Salvador's Coffee House.

Zhuhong had spent many years away from Bangdong, but in recent years he started making annual visits, bringing money and medicine for his parents. He knew how important a little supplemental income was for his family. He also knew that the problems facing his village required more than just money. Families needed a sustainable and secure future, one where parents could proudly raise children in the village and not worry that they were missing out on a better life in the city. Having returned to Bangdong, Zhuhong planned to do more than just bring gifts. He wanted to find a way to help the whole village.

Two days after our fortuitous meeting in Bangdong, Zhuhong visited us at one of our employee's homes where the parents had prepared a lunch for us. He proudly displayed in his hand a small rubber washer mended with beads of superglue. "I think I've fixed the clutch," he said smiling.

We didn't even know he was working on it, but he had managed to crawl under the car, undo some connections and discover that a tiny rubber washer had split, rendering the hydraulics in the 4x4's clutch useless. I could have spent a week taking the car apart and still would never have found the problem, but in village life people were used to being self-reliant. When a motorcycle or tractor breaks down far from any mechanic, people are left to fix it themselves. In the countryside, everything is DIY. If you don't do it yourself, there is no one else to do it for you.

Zhuhong was excited to see if his little repair would work. He took us back to the stranded vehicle, scooted underneath on his back, put all the parts back together and insisted we give it a try. A quick shift into first gear and then into reverse proved he had succeeded. The clutch was soft and still difficult to work, but at least it was good enough to turn the Jeep around and start back uphill.

We packed up our things and said goodbye to all of the families we had met. We still had five other families to meet in four different villages that day, so we got back on the road as soon as possible. We promised Zhuhong that we would pick him up later that day on the way back to Lincang's main city.

Every time we met the parents of our workers, they treated us with incredible kindness and generosity, and it was actually becoming uncomfortable. We had just wanted to stop by and say hello, and maybe sip on a little tea for a short chat, but every family we met refused to let us go until we had at least a quick meal. For them, if we didn't leave with full bellies, they had failed in their responsibilities as hosts. We did our best to refuse, but usually had no choice other than to relent.

After six hours and five family visits, our bellies were bulging with chicken soup, fried broccoli, boiled cabbage, fermented tofu, pickled mustard greens, salt-cured ham, handfuls of sunflower seeds and peanuts, and endless cups of tea. Luckily we were at least able to refuse alcohol because we were driving – if we hadn't, by the fifth household we would have been so tipsy that we would have been unable to find our feet, let alone our car keys.

Josh treated three different villagers during our time in the countryside. He used a combination of acupuncture and herbal medicines to treat one villager with a terrible flu and two with chronic joint problems. All three were genuinely thankful to have someone provide treatments they could not otherwise afford. Josh too found the treatments rewarding, as his skills proved more valuable to the villagers than they were to people in the city.

Over the course of our drive, Josh and I began discussing possible ways we could get involved with some sort of non-profit work in the villages. The Salvador's girls were far more than just our employees, and perhaps the bombing gave us an opportunity to be more than just a restaurant. In the villages, we could address health care issues. We could work with the school to promote education projects. We could work on sustainability issues or invest in crop development to increase family incomes. We were in a position to try anything, to experiment to see if there was any way we could be useful.

By the time we were ready to pick up Zhuhong on the way back to Lincang, we were excited to share with him some of our ideas. If we were to accomplish anything, we knew Zhuhong would be instrumental. The last thing we wanted to do was to strut about the village pretending like we knew what would be best for its residents. We needed to work with Zhuhong and to provide him with any necessary support.

When we told him about this, he looked at us as if we had read his mind. Together we hashed out our ideas for a new project we would call Village Progress. It would be the non-profit arm of Salvador's Coffee House. From then on, a percentage of profits from Salvador's would be used on initiatives to promote sustainable health care and education in Yunnan's countryside. And Bangdong would be where we tested our new ideas.

CHAPTER 19

AMERICAN DREAMS

"I need you to help me find someone in America to adopt my daughter," Mr. Wu told me, tears welling in his eyes. "I want her to grow up in America and go to American schools. I want her to have a better education than she would have with my wife and me."

I was caught completely off guard, and for a few moments was rendered speechless. "But she's only six years old," I said. "Isn't that a little young to leave her family?"

"It doesn't matter," he continued. "She deserves every opportunity she can get. Someday, I want her to be able to get into an American university."

I was shocked and saddened by the request. Mr. Wu and his wife were both schoolteachers and they had the highest aspirations for their daughter. For them, nothing was more important than education, but they lived in rural Yunnan and knew that village students rarely get an opportunity for higher education.

For many villagers in rural China, simply getting to the closest school means hiking for up to three hours. Because of this, students often live at the schools. Local governments sometimes pay for the students' room and board and even provide the family a monthly stipend to discourage youngsters from skipping school to help the family on the farm. The schools themselves are usually underfunded and struggle to hire good teachers and to pay for study materials. The result is that village students fall far behind city students, perpetuating a pattern that keeps them isolated and disadvantaged.

The Salvador's girls varied greatly when it came to their education levels. Many had received middle school educations, and a few graduated from high school, but some spent most of their childhood on the family farm away from school. One girl we hired, named A Shui, never learned to read or write Chinese in school. So in addition to her weekly English tutoring, she also received Chinese lessons from Naoko. Every week for nearly six months, Naoko taught her to read and write until she reached a level where she could take orders at the restaurant.

I'd known Mr. Wu for more than four years when he asked for my help with his daughter. I met him during my first year in Dali when a friend of mine had invited me to join her on a two-day trek in the mountains northwest of Dali. Mr. Wu lived in a satellite village of the larger town of Shaxi. It was nestled at the base of a large pine-forested mountain on one side and an expanse of wheat fields on the other. He had converted his home into a guesthouse that had solar-heated hot showers, a rarity in the countryside. The shower was just across from a small pen that housed a donkey who greeted visitors with rough, rasping brays.

When travelers came to his guesthouse, Mr. Wu guided them on hikes into the nearby mountain villages of Yi and Bai minorities. He had hiked just about every trail in the area and he was the only man around who knew them well enough to guide others. When I first met him he took me on a two-day hike that wound through tight valleys of pine forests following the path of the old Tea and Horse Caravan Road, a branch of the Southern Silk Road. We passed donkeys sluggishly hauling towering stacks of wood from the hillsides into town. The trail had been worn over centuries by the hooves of horses and mules that brought salt over from the next valley to Shaxi.

After a six-hour hike up a red clay slope, we arrived at the small village of Mapingguan. The high alpine gulch was lined with about 40 small wooden homes, in the middle of which was a covered wooden bridge that traders had used to cross the deep valley after paying a toll for passage.

This was all already ancient history when I visited the village for my first time, but Mapingguan still felt connected to the pre-modern age. There were no roads other than the steep mountain trail, so the village remained nearly as self-sufficient as it had been a century before. Cigarette butts and empty beer bottles were the only signs of an outside world. Nearly everything else was raised locally.

Mr. Wu led us to one home on the other side of the bridge where he had befriended a family the previous year. They welcomed us even though they were unprepared for our arrival. There were no phone lines at Mapingguan and cell phones were of little use so deep in the mountains, so communicating our arrival beforehand was not possible. They called us into their kitchen and asked us to sit near a small fire in the middle of the room. A chill filled the valley as the sun began to set, so the fire was warm and pleasant. The lady of the household had wrapped her long hair in a blue scarf atop her head, typical of many Bai minority women. She brought us a bowl of small purple potatoes to roast over the fire while she went to the courtyard to slaughter a chicken for our dinner.

Fire was vital to life in Mapingguan. Electric lines had yet to make their way up the hills to the village, so fire, obviously essential for cooking and lighting, also served as the centerpiece for evening conversation. This was something that had disappeared in many villages connected to the electrical grid, where televisions replaced the hearth. We sat with the grandfather and two younger sons of the household and snacked on fire-roasted potatoes while we waited for dinner.

In addition to a tasty braised chicken dish, dinner consisted of an assortment of wild mushrooms foraged from the nearby hills, a sautéed tree moss that had a pungent herbal flavor, and a homemade goat cheese – an unexpected treat that rivaled some blue cheeses from the West. Everything was grown or raised on the family farm or else gathered in the hills. It was a closed system and the kind of lifestyle I'd always aspired for: healthy, simple and sustainable. "If more places in the world were like this," I thought, "we'd live on a happier and healthier planet."

Why then, four years later, was Mr. Wu asking me to help him find a new home and family in the U.S. for his daughter? To me, life in the countryside was idyllic. If I had a child, I would wish him or her to experience the lifestyle of Mapingguan. But Mr. Wu wanted his daughter to experience the very lifestyle that I had longed to distance myself from.

It was the first time I realized how much I'd taken my childhood for granted. I had been lucky in life to get a full education and to have a world of opportunities open to me. While debating this with Mr. Wu, I started to understand how spoiled I'd been, and why Mr. Wu would go to such painful lengths to give his daughter the same opportunities that I'd had.

In the end, Mr. Wu changed his mind. He says that he realized that keeping the family together was far more important than his educational aspirations for his daughter. But the incident revealed just how trapped villagers sometimes feel. They know an entirely different world full of new opportunities is out there somewhere. But, no matter how unfair it might be, that world is off limits to them.

CHAPTER 20

A NEW DIRECTION

In 2010, Kris and I steered our roaring motorcycles into the front courtyard of the Bangdong Elementary School – the very same school Mengjuan, Zhuhong, Pingdi and a number of other Salvador's employees had attended as children. Excited students immediately tore out of their classrooms and ran in our direction. They clustered around us, laughing, cheering and unabashedly picking through our motorcycle gear – some strapping on the knee pads and helmets and others marveling at our bikes. For them, this was not a typical school day.

Aling had met us in the small town of Yunxian with an artist friend of hers named Yang Yang. Aling and Yang Yang rode on the motorcycles with us for the three-hour trip from Yunxian to Bangdong. Their backpacks were stuffed full of paints, brushes and markers, and they would give the students their first art lessons.

A Range Rover followed us into the schoolyard and soon all attention shifted from us to the tall, long-haired foreigner who stepped out of the rear door. At more than two meters tall, Gerry was not the typical sight in the countryside. The way the students marveled, he might as well have been Kobe Bryant. A number of the younger students ran up just to touch him, confirming that he was real, then giggled as they ran away.

Gerry was a wilderness survival specialist who had studied under Tom Brown Jr., one of the world's most respected survivalists. Gerry had come to Yunnan to study Chinese medicine and research traditional survival techniques among Yunnan's rural cultures. When he heard about our school art education project, he asked if he could join and offered to teach the kids some environmental awareness along with some fun survival skills.

Gerry stepped up onto a concrete platform, took out a chopstick-length stick, a small chunk of worn wood and some straw. A hush fell over the children as Gerry explained that he was going to show them how to make fire the way their ancestors did before the invention of matches or lighters. He placed the chunk of wood on the ground, took the stick between his two palms and started spinning it between his hands, driving it hard into the wood. After about 30 seconds a thin stream of smoke rose from the wood. Several children pointed excitedly. The smoke got thicker and thicker before Gerry cradled the ember into a small ball of tinder he had made from the straw. He raised it up into the air and softly blew into it. After a few delicate breaths, the tinder ball erupted into flames. The students cheered.

Now that he had the children's full attention, Gerry begin to explain the importance of protecting clean water resources. He even showed them how to make an impromptu water filter with a small piece of bamboo and some charcoal. The kids were enthralled by all of it.

Aling and Yang Yang then split up and took over two different classrooms to prepare for their art lessons. Children in the countryside are supposed to be guaranteed the same education as those in city schools. However, they rarely if ever get opportunities to work on creative projects. When I was young, I remember making collages from old magazines, creating macaroni animals with dried noodles and glue, painting messy pictures with my fingers and forming figurines with Play-Doh. These projects are more than just ways for teachers to use up school days. They help to stimulate imagination and creativity and see the world more colorfully.

Rural children in China often have responsibilities that include caring for livestock, tending crops and caring for younger siblings. Village parents work as many as 80 hours a week in the fields, so their children learn quickly how to care for themselves and for their siblings. School is the one place in the countryside where kids really get a chance to be kids.

In the future, we would redefine Village Progress to focus on schools. Simple school art and health projects did not require much money, which made them far easier to orchestrate. Aling and Yang Yang organized teams of artists and other volunteers willing to pay their own way for a chance to work with children while traveling through some of Yunnan's most stunning mountain landscapes.

At each school, the art teachers came up with projects using painting, drawing and collage. Meanwhile, Kris and I were responsible for incorporating health and safety education into lessons. Sometimes this meant finding volunteer doctors willing to join, but when they weren't available, Kris and I would interrupt each art class for 15 minutes to discuss nutrition and demonstrate simple first aid on our CPR dummy.

Most everything students learned in a full day of health and art education was new to them, and they appeared to take great interest in everything the teachers said. It was a rewarding experience for all of the volunteers, and we could only hope it was at least as rewarding for the students.

*   *   *

Cold rain drove into our faces like pins and needles. I tried pulling the helmet visor down, but every time I did so the rainwater dangerously blurred my vision. Kris and I ignored the pain of the needle-like raindrops and let our clothes get thoroughly soaked and our shoes fill with water.

Riding motorcycles at high speeds in a torrential rainstorm might not have been the best idea. The police escorts ahead of us, tasked with keeping us safe, did their best to convince us to leave the bikes and get in the car with them. A government van carried the rest of our team and we could have joined them in the warm dry vehicle. But for Kris and me, leaving the motorcycles behind was not an option. We had further roads to travel.

Kris and I joined three cardiologists and a police escort for the trip to Cangyuan near the Myanmar border. We joined with China California Heart Watch (ChinaCal), a non-profit that teaches village doctors about diagnosing and treating patients with high blood pressure and hypertension. Due to indoor smoke inhalation, along with a high consumption of salt, cigarettes and alcohol, heart disease is one of the main causes of death in China's villages. ChinaCal's goal was to give village doctors a step up on preventing this.

Village doctors in China are not too different from the 'barefoot doctors' of the past. They are usually local villagers who at some point received some basic medical training. They are the first line of defense for simple illnesses and injuries in the countryside, but they are often ill-equipped to give patients proper treatment.

We had just completed two clinics with 400 village doctors in the small cities of Lincang and Yunxian. At the expense of the Lincang health department, the village doctors had traveled from regional villages to participate in the ChinaCal training. Cangyuan would be the third stop on the trip, and there were another 150 village doctors awaiting us there.

The ChinaCal clinics consisted of lectures, written tests, hands-on training and role-playing exercises. Topics included patient assessment, preventative medications and how to improve patient diets. As non-medically-trained foreigners, our job was to entertain with games like 'Head, Shoulders, Knees and Toes' when lectures had students nodding off. When students looked especially bored, the clinic instructors would motion to Kris who would break out with a juggling routine, instantly bringing the audience back to life.

Village doctors attending the clinics ranged in age from 18 to 85. They were responsible for the health of more than 50,000 villagers in Lincang Prefecture. Some had traveled more than two days to attend. Many had only middle-school educations, while others had work experience in city hospitals. Some took the training very seriously, while others just used the clinics as a break from work. The diversity of the trainees made teaching more challenging, but the team from ChinaCal had years of experience teaching similar groups.

Six months earlier I had flown to Lincang to meet with the heads of Lincang's Health and Financial Departments with a proposal for the six-day clinic. After one day of meetings, and about 10 shots of rice wine, they agreed to finance the entire project. At a cost of nearly one million yuan (roughly $163,000), the government would cover all village doctor expenses for materials, transportation, food and accommodation.

Securing government funding for a project was a major step forward for Village Progress. Since Josh and I took that initial trip to Bangdong, we brought in a micro-financing expert to help us survey village economics. We brought a clean-burning stoves and sustainability expert. We had even tried bringing in a honey expert to see if the village had the potential for a poverty alleviation initiative. I wrote three separate grant proposals looking for funding for these projects. But after more than a year, Village Progress' financial situation was unsustainable. Funding was coming from restaurant profits and our own pockets. We knew that Village Progress would not survive long if that didn't change. The Lincang government's decision to fund the village doctor project gave us the motivation we needed for Village Progress to continue.

For six days Kris and I rode our motorcycles, often getting pounded by rain, to the clinics in Lincang, Yunxian and Cangyuan. Once they were all finished, we still had a four-day ride to get home. From Cangyuan we followed small roads along the Myanmar border, everything still soaking wet from riding through storms, and arrived at the small town of Mangkaba. After unpacking our bikes, we shot pool with some local kids, who proudly blasted Eminem and Green Day from their mobile phones. In soggy shoes and mildewed jeans, we toasted the end of our ride with a couple bottles of warm beer. An orange sunset reached across the sky, and the clouds looked particularly nice over Myanmar.

CHAPTER 21

Joining and Departing

A ling always knew what she wanted and was never shy about making
it happen. Her individual determination led her to leave her home
at the age of 14 in search of a new life. Her courage sustained her after
a terrible motorcycle accident suffered by her ex-boyfriend, in which he
lost all memory of her from head trauma. Her ambition made her one of
the most vocal and dedicated employees at Salvador's Coffee House. Her
ingenuity and creativity led to her impressive career as an artist. And on
July 23, 2011, her decisiveness led to suggesting that I should consider
proposing to her as we watched the sun set over the temple ruins at
Angkor Wat in Cambodia.

Our relationship was a bit different than what I would have envisioned
when I was younger. I had always thought that I'd marry some Colorado
mountain girl and we'd live in some remote mountain cabin. Instead, I
ended up with a very different kind of mountain girl and lived in a busy
city with close to 4 million other people. I spoke decent Chinese and
Aling spoke a bit of English, but talking about deep or important issues
was sometimes difficult. In some ways this made the relationship easier
as we never got too caught up in details, but sometimes communication
problems and cultural differences made our relationship feel distant.
After being together for six years we gained an understanding that went
beyond language and culture and we were able to relax into each other's
lives. It was then that we knew we could happily be together for the
foreseeable future.

My mother, an interfaith minister, was thrilled to help us organize a small wedding along a mountain creek in Steamboat Springs, Colorado. Ceremonies are not typically my kind of thing, but this one was perfect for Aling and me as it was small, simple and beautiful. My two brothers with their significant others accompanied my father alongside my mother as she conducted the ceremony. Aling was stunning in the flowing white dress she had made for herself. Our friend Vicky from Taiwan translated everything for her so that I could focus more on the task at hand. The creek behind us murmured softly as Aling and I embraced.

We celebrated the evening with live music and a feast of barbecue and cake. As Aling was welcomed into our family, she reflected on her own. She was nearly brought to tears as she told me how she wished her mother could have been there with us.

"Someday," she said, "we need to have another wedding in my village for my mother."

In the years leading up to our wedding, Aling's relationship with her mother had grown stronger than it ever was before. However, while they mended broken ties, her disdain for her father intensified, as seemingly every decision he made showed how irresponsible he'd become. This fact also wore on Aling's mother's patience with her husband and eventually led to their separation. They never divorced, and to some degree their lives remained intertwined, but they never again lived together.

In 2010, her father finally started making some smart business decisions again, and these earned him a good deal of cash. Unfortunately, old habits die hard. In one night he gambled it all away. Far worse, in a feverish attempt to win back his money, he borrowed more from some disreputable people. He quickly gambled that away as well.

While I was out on a trip in Lincang, Aling got a distressed phone call from her mother. She told Aling, about the gambling debt and that there was some concern for her father's health and well-being. Aling, along with her younger sister and brother, made a collective decision that this time he had gone too far and that they would not get involved. "Even if he dies, his life is no longer our concern. He's already dead to us," Aling told me.

Unbeknownst to Aling's mother, her father had already ingested a bottle of store-bought pesticide – apparently he had come to the same conclusion as his children and wished to end the burden he had brought upon his family. Four pain-filled days later, he died. Aling and her siblings were on the first overnight bus back to their parents' home. Their heavy hearts were full of sorrow and anger, yet mixed with a sense of relief that the perpetual suffering of their father was now over.

As is tradition, Aling's father was left in an open casket for three days in their home. It was the family's duty to watch over the body as other members of the family and the community came to pay their respects. Money collectors representing his creditors also came, but only to confirm his demise, not to mourn it.

Aling is not one who handles the physical aspect of death very well – a fact that became evident during our encounters with the dead at the burning ghats along the Ganges River on a trip in Varanasi, India. In Varanasi, bodies are ceremonially burned out in the open, something that was entirely inconsistent with Aling's worldview. However, in quiet observation of her father's body, she saw in his face a contentedness that she'd not seen since her childhood. "He looked happy," she said, "and I felt happy for him."

Funeral rites and rituals in China don't come cheap, and Aling felt the burden of her father's death fall squarely on her own shoulders. She knew that her mother and her siblings could not handle all of the financial responsibilities and funerary logistics on their own, and assumed that she would have to. She was pleasantly surprised when she arrived to find a very supportive village community comforting her mother, preparing the body, and even arranging burial.

Aling's village was only a 10-minute drive from one of Myanmar's border towns, making it a place where heroin is far more accessible than the rest of China. In addition to the typical alcohol and gambling addictions that plague rural Chinese communities, heroin too has torn apart many families in Aling's community. Because of this, people in her village seemed to easily look beyond individual failings. During a viewing of Aling's father's body, everyone in the village came to pay tribute to the man that Aling remembered from her youth, not the man who had gambled everything away.

Burial plots cost as much as 30,000 yuan (nearly $5,000), an amount that few rural families in Yunnan can afford, so most opt for cremation as a cheaper alternative. That is what Aling's family was planning to do as well, but her uncle already owned a burial plot in the village and offered it to the family free of charge. Others in the village took care of meals, cleaning, accounting and caring for her mother.

"I had no idea our village would treat us this way," Aling told me with tears in her eyes.

By the time I arrived at Aling's village, the body had already been moved to the burial site. Aling's family members, especially her mother, were in relatively good spirits. The tears had all been spilled and all that remained were memories.

A procession of visitors continued throughout the day. They thumbed through the collection of photos that Aling's mother had laminated in order to preserve them. Nearly all of the photos were of her children, and she was visibly proud when showing them to others. They laughed and poked fun at me every time they came across a photo of me. "I'm keeping this one," one woman said as she slipped one of these photos into her coat pocket, a devilish smile on her face.

There are times when China feels overly sanitized and emotionless. Change has come so fast, especially to the cities, that compassion often makes way for survival. The experience with the funeral reminded me that that there was still much about the culture I had yet to grasp. Compassion was everywhere, it just revealed itself so much differently than what I was used to. Especially in the countryside, it seemed that when help was most needed, it arrived with a smile.

As is the tradition, we shared one last meal with her father at his burial site. An assortment of meat and vegetable dishes, fresh fruits, hot tea, a glass of corn liquor and a lit cigarette were all placed at the head of his grave so that he would not feel hunger when he departed this world. Spirit money, a printed currency meant for use in the afterlife, was burned to assure he left with wealth. His bed, clothes and belongings, including a leather handbag full of gambling ticket stubs, were all put into a large pile and set ablaze.

I sat alongside Aling's mother, sister, brother and uncle in the small field. The nearby sugarcane fields creaked and swayed as we snacked on pears and oranges. I was privileged to have been a part of the ceremony and felt at home with the family. It was a beautiful way to say goodbye to Aling's father as the last traces of his life burned away in a curling trail of thick, black smoke.

CHAPTER 22

SCENE OF THE CRIME

"Li Yan was not from Xuanwei," Qin Hui insisted. "That *gouri* ('dog dick') came from Huize."

Qin Hui went through all of the old newspaper clippings about the Salvador's bomber with me, he made sure that I clearly understood the fact that Li Yan, the man who detonated the bomb in Salvador's in 2008, did not come from his hometown.

Though most of Li Yan's youth was spent in Xuanwei, he was actually an outsider, born in another town four hours to the north. His parents divorced when he was 10, and he moved with his father to Xuanwei. Li Yan told everyone that he met in his new school that he was an orphan whose parents had died.

Li Yan was a troubled kid and often acted out violently in school. He was once suspended for dumping a pot of boiling water on a girl who had teased him, and when he started middle school at age 12 he only lasted three days before dropping out. He then wandered from town to town, stealing, fighting and causing trouble. By age 15, he was a professional criminal, something that earned him the trust of some local mafia. For the next three years, Li Yan went around to brothels and underground casinos collecting dues owed to his bosses. It was a violent profession that earned him the name, Xiao Haoshan (小浩山), a name often reserved for people of great importance.

In 2001, the law finally caught up to Li Yan. He was arrested for robbery, property damage and assault and sentenced to nine years in prison. In prison, he learned to be an electrician, and it is likely there that he learned to make bombs.

After nearly five years, Li Yan was released early for good behavior. He found a job working for a highway construction company and made his way up the ranks to a management position. His boss entrusted him with large cash amounts to make equipment purchases in Kunming. It was later discovered that Li Yan had in fact been embezzling his boss's money and equipment. The day of the Salvador's bombing, he was given 20,000 yuan to buy construction materials in Kunming. It was that money, along with Li Yan's blood and body parts, that had been strewn over the first floor of Salvador's.

As Qin Hui relayed Li Yan's story to me, I couldn't help but think of Zhuhong, our friend from Bangdong. He too had grown up as a troubled youth and had been a violent enforcer for the mafia before getting caught by the police. The two led such similar early lives and it had me questioning what had made their adult lives take such different courses. Zhuhong was just about the nicest person I'd ever met, so how the hell did Li Yan turn out to be such a 'dog dick?' It was that question that brought me to Xuanwei.

Xuanwei, a booming coal town in northern Yunnan Province, is about a three-hour drive from Kunming. Other than coal, the town is mostly known for its dry-cured ham and as the birthplace of Zhou Lin, the late wife of Deng Xiaoping, former leader of the Communist Party of China.

The drive from Kunming to Xuanwei follows a road along craggy hills. Overfilled trucks from the mines around Xuanwei spill small chunks of coal onto the highway with every little bump in the road. A thick layer of black dust covers everything and passing cars kick up clouds of the stuff, making an otherwise lovely drive difficult and unpleasant.

About five kilometers before the town, six large chimneys from the Xuanwei Power Plant come into view. The dark smoke they spit into the sky blows out over the nearby hillside. Coal accounts for close to 75 percent of China's total power generation, and Xuanwei's mining industry works feverishly to keep up with growing energy demands. Consequently, Xuanwei now has one of the highest rates of lung cancer in China.

Four years after Li Yan's death I drove to Xuanwei to see where Li Yan came from. I hoped to understand what shaped him, what made him hate the world enough to wreak havoc upon it. I envisioned dirt roads and destitute folks feeling stuck in their dirty coal town. I imagined we would walk along decrepit sidewalks investigating where Li Yan grew up. Maybe I could visit his school, or the bus station where his father worked. Perhaps we would find some of his friends or family and reminisce about where and when Li Yan's life took a violent turn. I wanted to find some sort of meaning in the man's senseless actions, and perhaps find some sort of closure.

Li Yan's death and his violent actions at Salvador's had taken its toll on me. My disturbing daydreams were no longer as frequent or as dramatic, but by all accounts I was a different person. I'd get very uncomfortable when Salvador's would fill up with customers, especially when some of them started getting drunk. The business and drunkenness always had me feeling anxious, like something bad was about to happen. Soon, every time Salvador's started getting really busy, I had to leave. Eventually I just got in the habit of leaving Salvador's by dinner time and not returning till morning, in order to avoid the crowds.

I also stopped going out with friends at night, as the combination of crowds and alcohol in other bars had a similar effect. Friends told me that it seemed I'd forgotten how to have fun. It was a problem that I tried to fix with more traveling and motorcycle adventures, but there was nothing that seemed to get me excited anymore. Instead, I put all of my energy into work: fundraising for Village Progress and trying to make Salvador's better and more profitable. To many, it seemed that all I did was work.

The more I focused on projects, the more my friendships dissolved. Josh, Naoko, Kris and I found ourselves increasingly distanced from one another and more often at odds than in agreement. My obsession with work had me full-steam ahead on new ideas and changes for Salvador's and Village Progress, and I was becoming aggressive and overbearing with my opinions. The more I pushed, the less interested they became.

My relationship with Aling also suffered as I buried myself in work and new responsibilities. I would come home early, sit at the computer to work and barely say a word until bed time. Our relationship lost some of its excitement and I was becoming a bore.

I needed a reboot and change of lifestyle. I needed to find a way to put Li Yan behind me and move on. That's why I went to Xuanwei, to try and piece things back together. Kris and Aling came with me on the two-day drive.

For the last hour of the drive to Xuanwei, we slowly worked through traffic along a road covered in coal dust. We had to roll up the car windows as the filthy air burned our eyes and throats. As we passed the power plant, the road opened up into a large flat valley. I thought Xuanwei would be filled with the drab gray concrete buildings typical of many poorer Chinese towns. Instead, we saw modern high-rise buildings towering over the town, and it was apparent that it was not so destitute after all. There were still plenty of ugly apartment blocks, but interspersed throughout were signs of modernization.

At the very edge of town, a multitude of car washes greeted vehicles and sprayed away the dirt into dark black puddles. The car-washes served as a kind of border between the ravages of the coal industry and a town that was, by contrast, nice and clean. Xuanwei was full of busy noodle stalls, flower vendors, fruit stands, hotels, property management offices, grocers, toy shops and bakeries. The town was not quite the slum I had expected.

After checking into our hotel, we flagged down a taxi to take us to the bus station where Li Yan's father had worked. The driver of the taxi was a woman of about 40 named Mrs. Ling.

"It will cost you 10 renminbi to get there," she said. "But you won't find anything. The station moved a couple years back."

"Are you native to Xuanwei?" I asked.

"Yes, but I grew up closer to the power plant."

"What was that like?"

"Terrible," she said. "Sometimes the wind would change direction and everything would get covered with soot. But Xuanwei has changed a lot since those days."

Mrs. Ling pointed to all the buildings along the main road. "This was all farmland 10 years ago. Really, most of this city was farmland back then."

We asked Mrs. Ling to take some detours and show us more of the city. She insisted that there was nothing special about Xuanwei but agreed to do so anyway.

She was right. It was just another Chinese town. Xuanwei had hit the reset button, and like so many other Chinese towns, the past had been erased with bulldozers and buried by concrete. Xuanwei was full of ambition, with little reverence for its own history. It had succeeded in growing from a large village into a lively town in less than a decade.

It's always remarkable to witness how quickly change happens in China. Xuanwei is only one of thousands of cities that had experienced the same rush to modernize. China has spent much of the past half-century reinventing itself. This usually came in the form of demolition and rebuilding. During the Cultural Revolution a common slogan was, "Destroy the old world. Forge the new world." Today this idea continues with new fervor, albeit with less violence.

In just about every city or town in China, it's common to see the character 拆 spray-painted all over storefronts and apartment buildings. The word, chai, means, "demolish," and wherever it is painted, the demolition countdown is already underway. Chinese developers often plow right through residential areas to lay new highways, railroads, malls or other development projects. There is a running joke about the phrase, "*chai na?*" – pronounced the same as *China* – which more or less means, "What should we knock down next?"

A number of times I've witnessed residents refuse to leave their homes even as the bulldozers wait outside. Sometimes such standoffs can last months with government forces either finally evicting residents physically or, less commonly, relenting to resident demands.

For example, in 2006, the Kunming government began construction on Wenlin Jie, a small road that runs perpendicular to the lane where Salvador's is located. There were plans to widen the road in order to accommodate increased traffic. It took more than a year to get most of the residents to accept compensation and leave, so that road crews could level their homes. One little building that housed two noodle shops, a convenience store and a small toy store refused to close. After several months, road crews decided to leave the building alone. Now, years later, the small crooked building still juts out into the street.

Mrs. Ling drove us to the old bus station where Li Yan's father was once employed. At one time, it served as the town's center, but the bus station had long been abandoned. Xuanwei had built a new station in another part of the city, leaving the old one to weather away. Now it stood as nothing more than a stained concrete structure scarred with broken windows. A row of men with bicycle carts waited at the gate, hoping to get hired as day laborers.

"Why would you want to come here anyway?" Mrs. Ling asked. I wasn't sure if by "here" she meant the bus station or Xuanwei, but we told her about Li Yan and the bombing at our café.

"I had no idea he was from Xuanwei," she told us. "I was in Kunming visiting my brother the day of the bus bombings. I was only a couple of blocks away. I don't understand why anyone would want to do that."

It was becoming clear to me that, no matter whom I talked to, I was never going to understand why either. I could try to put meaning to Li Yan's actions. I could imagine that maybe he was never accepted in Xuanwei because he'd only moved there when he was a child. I could guess that maybe the other kids made fun of him. I could guess that maybe his family was poorer and more disenfranchised than many in Xuanwei and that Li Yan grew to despise those more fortunate than him. I could guess that maybe his father was too busy with work to serve as a good parent, resulting in Li Yan's violent tendencies. But such ideas only put false meaning to what was likely nothing more than the deranged actions of a deranged man.

At night, Kris and I walked over to the town's public square. Public squares in China serve as places for people to gather for exercising, dancing, singing or chatting with friends or neighbors. Most public squares in China are merely worn concrete spaces lined with sparse trees and bushes, but Xuanwei's new public square that was something totally different. Instead of a square it was actually an enormous circle tiled with granite and laced with cobbled paths where older people could walk barefoot to massage their feet. A large natural rock outcropping lined the back of the square and trails went off in a number of directions into small forests.

The square that night was filled with people. Couples walked hand in hand. Children played with remote-controlled cars. Groups of young men watched groups of young women, each side too shy to approach the other. And a gathering of about 40 elderly couples were learning to dance the foxtrot.

We walked along the back of the square into a kind of festival grounds where the smell of cotton candy filled the air. Children sat in large sand boxes gleefully scooping the sand into small mounds with miniature tractors and back-hoes. An inflated pool was filled with frogs and tadpoles and surrounded by kids trying to catch them in little nets.

We took seats outside a nearby bar and sipped on warm beers, watching the people pass by. This was not the Xuanwei I had expected. It was pleasant and lively, and Kris and I had one of those special moments in China where we just sat back and watched it happen.

We'd been at the bar for only about 10 minutes when a young man approached us, holding a full glass of wine. He asked in his best English if we could speak Chinese. He smiled and sighed with relief when we said we could.

"Please join me and my friends inside," he said. "We rarely get the opportunity to drink with foreigners."

Kris and I looked at each other and shrugged. "Why not?" I said.

Inside we sat at a large table with eight men and women all in their twenties. They spent the next hour pouring glass after glass of sour Chinese red wine and teaching us different drinking games. One was a team version of rock, paper, scissors, in which the losing team had to drink. Another game was faster-paced and required hand signals that represented the numbers one through five. Two beat one, three beat two, four beat three, five beat four and one beat five. It seemed simple enough, but we were no match for their practiced techniques.

"We get bored here in Xuanwei sometimes," one of the girls said to me. "So you have to understand how nice it is to meet you guys. I went to college in Lijiang and I used to see foreigners all the time. But since I moved back home to Xuanwei, that never happens anymore."

We clinked wine glasses again and took a sip.

"What brings you here anyway?" asked the one who invited us in, as he offered us a plate of spicy fried potatoes.

It seemed like a buzz kill to interject Li Yan into the conversation, but that was what we were there for, so we told him about Salvador's and the bombing four years earlier. His eyes softened and his big smile melted away. "I'm really sorry," he said wholeheartedly.

Obviously there was no reason for him to apologize and we quickly made that fact clear to him. But in a kind of selfish way, I think it was what I went to Xuanwei to hear. I had made the mistake of thinking that Li Yan must have in some way been a product of Xuanwei. In trying to find reason, I convinced myself believe that it was the town that had made him into the villain that bombed us. The sincerity behind our new friend's apology only revealed my own ignorance. Li Yan may have grown up alongside the nice young man at the bar, but the two probably had less in common than I did with our new friends.

Many of the girls at Salvador's had grown up in troubled families. Alcoholism, gambling and even physical abuse were issues for many of them. Yaya's youth was made difficult by the fact that she had to shoulder much of the burden of her parents' disabilities. The family was dependent upon their tea, corn and rice harvests, so Yaya toiled at home and in the fields to provide for her family. But she had come to Kunming more humbled by her hard life than tortured by it.

Yaya, the employee who joined us after A Li's wedding, was arguably one of the slowest workers we had ever hired. A number of times other girls approached me worrying that perhaps Yaya wasn't cut out for the work. However, over eight years, and the employment of more than 50 young women from the countryside, we learned that sometimes the most reliable employees take time to adjust. The payoff comes when girls like Yaya realize just how capable they are.

Perhaps Li Yan was never given the opportunity that Yaya was. If he had, maybe things would have turned out differently. For years I tried to sympathize with Li Yan and understand why he did what he did. I even started thinking of him as the victim, and that what he'd become was not his fault. That line of thought needed to change. The choices he made in his miserable life, and even more miserable death, were not my responsibility. Nor did I owe him any pity.

As we drove back to Kunming from Xuanwei, I thought back to the day of the bombing, back to when the medics brought us to the rear of the ambulance to see Li Yan's mangled body. I remember looking into his dazed eyes – life draining away – feeling he was trying to say something.

Four years later, I told myself to accept that brief moment between us as his apology.

CHAPTER 23

THE ART OF BAKING BREAD

Li Ping had only been working at Salvador's for eight months when we learned that her kidneys were failing. She was only 17 years old.

She had grown up in Dalubian in a small home next to A Li, about a 15 minute walk from Yaya's home. When Li Ping first came to Salvador's early in 2012, we saw in her eyes the same timidity that Yaya carried with her the day she left with us from her village. And similar to when Yaya came to Salvador's, the other girls didn't think Li Ping had what it took to work for us. During her first six months she frequently messed up orders, she was painfully slow in the kitchen and sometimes just seemed to be totally out of it, mesmerized by everything going on around her.

This happened with nearly every girl who came to Salvador's. They arrived in a city that in no way resembled the world they had left behind. Then they were taught to make cappuccinos and Greek salads and trained to interact with the customers. It was always a bit disorienting at first, but somewhere between two and six months into working at Salvador's, a light suddenly switches on, as if they had been shocked into consciousness. Their eyes widen, they smile more, they stand up straighter and they go about their work with pride and motivation. Like Yaya before her, it took Li Ping longer than most for that light to switch on.

One day about six months into Li Ping's employment, the other girls called me into the kitchen. They told me that Li Ping wanted to show me something but she was too shy to say so. One of the girls behind Li Ping nudged her forward with her elbow, goading her to speak up.

"I… I baked some bread," she said blushing, looking down at her feet.

The kitchen manager, beaming with pride for her protégé, lifted the baking tray from the cooling rack to show me. Two perfect loaves of whole wheat oat bread bulged out of their metal pans. The crust was golden brown and carefully decorated with oat flakes. The sweet smell of freshly baked bread filled the kitchen.

"Wow," I said patting her on her shoulder. "Those are perfect. Good job."

The other girls giggled as Li Ping's face reddened.

After eight months with us, Li Ping had established herself as a good waitress, baker and barista. She was in the process of earning her promotion as a chef when our manager informed me that Li Ping was ill and might need a couple of days off. We granted the request but assumed she had just caught the cold that had been going around. Two days later, however, A Li said Li Ping was actually very sick and would need to return home to her village.

Li Ping's kidneys were failing and the doctors in Kunming had told her that there wasn't much they could do. What that meant, however, was that there wasn't much that they could do that Li Ping could afford.

For those with rural health insurance, only a fraction of treatment at city hospitals is covered. We were assured that if Li Ping returned to Lincang, her parents would meet her at the bus station in the town nearest her home. There, her rural insurance could cover more of her medical costs at the local hospital. We concurred and she boarded a bus for home. The next day we learned the unfortunate news that instead of taking her to the hospital, the family had taken her back to the village.

When Li Ping's kidneys stopped working altogether, her body started accumulating excess water and toxins. She was no longer receiving the nutrients necessary for normal body functions and without immediate dialysis she would die. The village was an hour's motorcycle ride from the nearest main road and then another hour bus ride to the nearest medical facility with dialysis machines. If she stayed in the village much longer she would die.

We assumed that Li Ping's parents had not fully understood the gravity of the situation so we asked A Li to contact them and explain the urgency of Li Ping's illness. A Li had been our manager for more than seven years and was like an older sister to many of the girls, but for Li Ping the connection was much deeper as they were related by blood.

A Li did her best to convince Li Ping's parents to get her to a hospital. They told her that they had "*fangqi-le*" – given up. This was a new phrase for me in Chinese. Once I understood the meaning, I still could not understand how they could reach such a decision. There were options available to keep their daughter alive, but they had made the decision that she would die at home.

Through A Li, we continued trying to persuade the parents to release their daughter to us. We offered to drive the 10 hours to come pick her up and bring her back to Kunming for treatment. We would find a way to deal with the financial issues later.

All of our hopes were crushed after A Li spoke directly to Li Ping. She also declared she had "*fangqi-le.*"

The phrase *fangqi-le* repeated on a loop in my head. It was a phrase filled with hopelessness and it deflated any optimism we had for Li Ping's recovery. Aling did her best to help me understand that this was normal in village life. There comes a point when treatment is just too costly and village families accept death as the only pragmatic option.

This was the painful truth in the countryside, and I was not prepared for it. None of us were. Never before had I had to stand idly by while a friend died just because of the financial burden that treatment would incur, but our hands were tied. None of us wanted to live with the guilt of doing nothing while someone we cared about died, but we also couldn't just go and kidnap her to take her to the hospital. It was not our place to do so. We would have to do our best to convince ourselves that the decision was not ours to make.

It was both a shock and a relief to get a phone call from A Li the next day saying that Li Ping and her parents had boarded a bus bound for Kunming earlier that morning. We were elated and all the pain and frustration we faced instantly melted away. We were also faced with the fact that we were now responsible for Li Ping's survival. Approaching our new responsibility with anything but our full commitment could have dire consequences.

We contacted a friend from China California Heart Watch whom we had worked with on the Lincang village doctor training project. They referred us to a hospital that specialized in kidney treatment and helped us to contact the head physicians in order to arrange a bed for Li Ping. It was a valuable referral that helped us find the right place for treatment in a city with many hospitals to choose from.

Josh and I greeted Li Ping at the hospital. Her face was bloated and her skin pale and yellow. She was conscious, but exhausted and delirious, yet she still managed to give us a quick smile. Doctors immediately got her on diuretic medications to try and eliminate some of the dangerous toxic fluids building up in her body. They then scheduled her for the first of three dialysis treatments she would receive that week.

The doctors warned us that the worst-case scenario was also the most likely. She had chronic renal failure and would almost certainly require dialysis at least twice a week for the rest of her life. At more than $5,000 per year, this was a cost that Li Ping's family could not afford. For them, this was basically a death sentence.

We spread word of Li Ping's situation to our customers in Kunming and to our friends and families abroad. Using all of the social media at our disposal, we launched a fundraiser to try and cover as much of the medical expenses as we could. By the end of the first week we had already raised nearly $8,000. It was an amazing start, but only barely enough to get her through a year and a half of treatments.

"Then what?" we all asked ourselves. Her family's difficult situation would be no different a year and a half later. We had started something and we would have to stay with it for the long run. We could not just hand over a chunk of money to Li Ping and her family and say, "Good luck."

There were many others in China like Li Ping who could not afford life-saving medical treatment. Our goal with Village Progress was to do what we could to address this issue, though in a very small way. Li Ping's medical situation presented a more immediate problem and we were scrambling to solve it. Luckily for us, friends, family and the people of Kunming were ready to stand behind Li Ping.

Over the next four months we set a goal to raise $24,000 to cover Li Ping's first five years of treatment. We had managed to raise only about $4,000 for Village Progress over the past two years, but for Li Ping, the money came in more easily. People who had never met her, or had even been to Salvador's, were ready to support Li Ping financially.

John Lundemo, known to all of us in Kunming as Nevada, had been teaching English and playing music in Kunming for more than five years when Li Ping got sick. He knew the girls by name and they were used to his unabashed and often slightly inebriated teasing. He was a blues and rock musician who lived true to the classic rock star lifestyle and his thinned mop of white hair flowed wherever the wind was blowing. He is about as kindhearted as anyone can be and he took to the Li Ping fundraising effort with a strong hand and heart.

Nevada organized his band, War Whores, and four other bands to perform free of charge at a benefit concert. Tickets were sold at 30 yuan ($4.50), and Nevada made sure that everyone bought tickets. Many even bought them knowing full-well they would be unable to attend the event. Nevada's benefit concert raised more than $1,000 for Li Ping.

Slice of Heaven, a bakery and café owned by Barbara Duff, an impassioned woman from New Zealand, organized her own fundraiser, raising another $400. The Go Kunming website made a promotion for ad space with proceeds going to the fund for Li Ping. Other expats also joined in with their own fundraising ideas and donations.

Generous donations also poured in from locals. Yunnan Spring Water, one of China's largest mineral water companies, got word of the fundraiser from Go Kunming. They donated 300 cases of water and organized a local media interview. Over the next few weeks, locals who had never even heard of Salvador's before came with donations up to $300 each and took only a bottle or a case of water in return.

It was an amazing turnout, and the result was that we hit our fundraising target of $24,000 in four months. I had decided on that target rather haphazardly, assuming that it would be good to pursue a number higher than we were capable of raising in order to emphasize how dire the situation was. I never thought we could find that much money so quickly. The Salvador's community and the extended community beyond Kunming proved far more generous and caring than we ever could have expected.

Li Ping recovered her health and her strength. She went back to work on the farm and made the four-hour round-trip to the hospital twice a week for dialysis. When I returned to her village, the same village where A Li was married six years earlier, Li Ping looked just like any healthy girl her age. Even when she first came to Salvador's she had had an odd-shaped face and chubby figure, probably because her kidneys were already stressed, making her body bloated. But after the treatment, she looked far better. She was slender and had a healthy complexion.

She took me on a short hike up the hillside into the tea farms. Though we talked some, most of the time she was looking at her phone and texting messages to her friends. I wasn't offended as it was nice to see her living the life of a typical teenager.

It was unlikely that Li Ping would ever return to work with us at Salvador's. She would stay with her family and return to the life of a farming girl. For the foreseeable future, she would make the long trip for her treatments twice a week. We hoped that she would live like any other young woman for the other five days.

According to the doctors, a kidney transplant was not an option for Li Ping. Her heart had already suffered too much trauma from the initial illness. Even if she survived a transplant, the medications needed for the rest of her life would be even more expensive than dialysis. So with enough money to cover her next five years of treatment, we relaxed with the knowledge of Li Ping's secure future.

For the first nine months, treatment seemed to be going smoothly as our fundraising pursuits continued. Nevada and Barbara teamed up with some other friends for another concert fundraiser at Slice of Heaven that raised more than $2,000. Salvador's customers also continued to give donations. So early in July of 2013, it was shocking to get a phone call from A Li telling me that we should stop the fundraiser and start returning money to donors.

"She doesn't need it now," she said in a somber tone. "I hope the donors aren't angry."

I was still trying to figure out what she was trying to say, so I asked, "Why? What happened?" But as soon as those words passed my mouth, I figured it out.

"She is no longer here," A Li said. "She was on her way to the hospital, but there were complications."

Li Ping died from heart failure. She was on the way down the mountain with her father to go for dialysis treatment when she collapsed. With some help, her father carried her back up to their home. Two hours later her heart stopped beating and she died.

The news was a shock.

I had talked with Li Ping only a couple of weeks earlier about coming out to Kunming to meet with some new doctors to see if there were any other options to make her life easier. She seemed to be in relatively good spirits, but clearly her heart had weakened to a point where it could take no more.

We considered closing Salvador's to travel together to her funeral, but A Li told me that we should not go. She told me that in this kind of situation, our presence would bring more pain than relief to her family. Instead, A Li tasked me with a mission to contact everyone who had donated money in order to tell them of the tragic loss and return their money.

Upon hearing the news, no donors asked for their money back. Instead, they encouraged us to support others like Li Ping who could not afford needed health care. It was the consensus of everyone that, in Li Ping's name, the fundraiser effort should go on.

The next time I saw Nevada, I could barely hold back my tears as we talked about what had happened. But at the end of the conversation, Nevada started planning for the next benefit concert.

CHAPTER 24

DIRT DUMPLINGS

In Yaya's small mountain village in Lincang, dirt trails were the only link between neighbors and villages. From her home she could see over three different valleys far into the distance, but in Kunming she was suddenly in a world of traffic jams and high-rises. When Yaya stepped off the bus with us in Kunming, she entered a new world.

In many ways, Kunming was more foreign to her than it was to me – I grew up with cars, elevators, fast-food and crosswalks. I could walk into any city in the world and find a way to get food and shelter, and seek help if necessary. When I arrived in Kunming, I possessed the basic understanding of how cities function. For Yaya, Kunming was far more alien.

Yaya had never even been more than five kilometers from her home. For her first few weeks in Kunming, she desperately missed her mother. She had never used public transportation before, never even boarding a bus or car of any kind. And now she had to learn to navigate a large city with over a hundred different bus routes.

Yaya is only one of nearly 150 million Chinese who moved from the countryside to urban areas since 1980. China's urban population boom hasn't come from a high birth rate, but from people leaving the surrounding countryside for the city. As China softened its stance on the household registration system in the late 1990s and people had more freedom to move about the country, farmers put down their plows and ventured to cities with dreams of making it big. Every city in the country quickly became a haven of migrant laborers.

"Kunming is a city of dirt dumplings," Qin Hui once told me. What he meant by that was that Kunming was a city full of villagers.

Tubaozi is an offensive term urbanites use to degrade country folk who move into the cities from the countryside. Qin Hui, however, used it with a more jovial intention. He had even nicknamed his best friend, Tubaozi. It was a name that stuck to the point that most never learned his real name.

Qin Hui was also born into a farming family and moved to Kunming in search of something more than the farm offered. In fact, most of my Chinese friends in Kunming could be considered 'dirt dumplings' as the majority of them came from villages throughout China and had come to Kunming either on their own or with their families. Like most rural-to-urban migrants, they too have their own stories about surviving the move to Kunming as cities are not always so welcoming to newcomers.

Much like the villagers who had to make way for the giant Three Gorges Reservoir experienced, the transition to city life was difficult. Not only did they lose their self-sustainability by leaving the farm behind, they also lost their social networks.

Millions in China have left their families behind and given up the quiet of the village. No longer do they wake up early to walk the geese to the pond or take the goats out to pasture. In the city they must buy groceries at the market instead of walking out to the fields to find the ripest fruits and vegetables.

In the city, they realize that for the first time in their lives, they are completely on their own. They find themselves in the middle of an urban rat race – a race to make money, a race to find a husband or a wife, a race to get on the bus before it fills up and a race to get through dense traffic for a job on the other side of town.

Many migrants who choose to move to cities hoping to improve their quality of life and that of their children find themselves worse off than they would have been back in the village. These new arrivals frequently have little or no education. The many skills that might serve them well in the countryside have little value in the city. Their heavy accents and countryside manners make finding work in the city much more difficult. And the discrimination some experience because of ethnicity or dark skin complicates things further.

Instead of fulfilling their dreams, many end up as factory workers, assembling athletic shoes for 80 hours a week, or as low-level construction workers getting paid little for high-risk jobs. Some get involved in prostitution and gambling, while others fall into drug and alcohol addiction. The result is that many are unable to make it in the city and they eventually return to their villages. Some who stay, do eventually find their place. Cities like Kunming have quickly developed into large urban centers heavily populated by people who came from farming communities.

When outsiders hear about urban China, they hear about pollution, overpopulation, heavy traffic, mass consumerism and a blind rush toward modernization. Though all of those characterizations are often what people experience when they come to China, many millions of rural Chinese think of China's cities in a very different context. For them, cities are the gateways to the modern world.

Most Chinese will say that life in the countryside is *xinku*, or "hard working." Young migrants expect to find city life easier than farm life. They hope to make money for their futures, and a little extra to send back to family in the village. And once they have children of their own, they expect them to get better schooling in the city than they would in the village. However, the economic inequality in cities between migrant workers and wealthier urbanites grows exponentially.

Some migrants dig through trash piles behind swanky golf resorts to find anything recyclable that can be sold. Others find any available patch of unclaimed land to plant vegetables in order to avoid rising food costs and retain a small connection to their farm. And many buy fruits and vegetables from unregistered farmers to sell them on the streets at prices that undercut legal vendors.

In most Chinese cities, cheap produce is a black market commodity. Throughout Kunming, illegal vendors can be seen pushing small carts full of fruits, vegetables and other goods. In an effort to curb this trend, the city's urban planning police force, called *chengguan*, attempts to control these vendors. They spend their days chasing illegal produce carts all over the city and confiscating them when possible. This often fuels confrontations that have a tendency to turn violent, and as the number of such vendors grows, these battles escalate.

Just a few months after we first opened Salvador's Coffee House in Kunming, a scuffle broke out just outside our front door between an illegal potato vendor and a *chengguan* officer. The officer was trying to confiscate the illegal goods but the vendor refused. The officer grabbed the cart carrying the potatoes and pulled it away from the vendor. The vendor took out a knife, tackled the officer into our outdoor tables and plunged the knife into the officer's stomach. The officer later died from the wounds and our traumatized manager had to be a witness in the court hearings where the vendor was sentenced to life in prison. Though these scuffles rarely end so tragically, they are still frequent.

Chinese cities change at a pace unlike the world has ever seen. Kunming has installed a brand new international airport, a new subway system, scores of towering apartments and a number of huge malls with 3D movie theaters. There is very little about the city that is not new.

Whenever I join Wang Hu in his black Jeep Cherokee for a ride across town, it is astonishing to hear what Kunming was like when he was a kid. Many of his memories are clouded by the hardships his family suffered to survive the turmoil of the 60s and 70s. "When I see video of what North Korea is like now," Wang Hu told me, "I am reminded of what China was like when I was a kid. We rarely had enough to eat but any criticism of those in charge was met with harsh punishment."

Wang Hu used to ride his bike to nearby Dianchi Lake where he could swim and fish in the clean water. Present-day Dianchi Lake, however, has been suffocated by a nasty plague of seaweed. After years of runoff from phosphate-filled fertilizers and potassium-laden detergents, the seaweed bloomed and sucked out all of the oxygen, killing off all of the animal life and converting China's fourth largest lake into a cesspool of green slime.

Even the changes that Kunming has undergone over the 10 years that I have lived here are stupefying. Areas that were farmland when I first came have been converted into residential and commercial areas. The city has actually grown in size by more than five times over 10 years. Roads have gone from empty of anything but sparse taxis and buses to being packed full of traffic – taxi drivers used to race through the city with glee but now compete with the 700 cars added to the city's roads every day.

Nevertheless, no matter what physical changes come to Kunming, the pervasive culture of the city is still that of the farmer. People still ride their donkey carts onto the main roads. Knife sharpeners still drag around their stone wheel and announce their presence with loud chants. Parents potty-train their children in public view in the middle of the sidewalk, and most still don't use diapers. Many shoppers would rather buy a live chicken than a butchered one. Even the 20th floor of an apartment building isn't safe from the ruckus of early morning rooster calls as neighbors often raise chickens out on the balcony.

Kunming's social strata range from those with extreme wealth to those in extreme poverty – obvious in what people drive, where they live, what they wear, what they eat, where their children go to school and what kind of medical care they get. Migrants make their homes in shabby apartment buildings just around the corner from swanky clubs where the wealthy sip on 12-year-old Scotches, Turkish-style bathhouses where men get pedicures and exfoliating scrubs, and fancy malls where high-heeled women carrying Prada handbags shop the most expensive brands. The wealthy drive fancy new cars to one of the many high-end golf courses opened in Kunming over the past 10 years, while some migrants can't even afford basic medical care. Donkey-pulled fruit carts use the same roads as brand new Maseratis and Lamborghinis – more proof that Kunming, like many other cities in China, has become a convergence point for two very different worlds.

In past years, when a girl from the countryside came to work at Salvador's, one of the first things she would do with her first paycheck is buy a new mobile phone. It is an instant source of pride for her. The phone is a symbolic step toward independence, and one stride in the great race to becoming an urbanite. New clothes and new shoes soon follow. She is introduced to the Internet and gets on QQ, a social media site where people can meet new people in chat rooms. A few of the girls have found their boyfriends, and even husbands, this way.

I will admit that I never much liked cities, feeling that they are just the unfortunate side effects of our modernizing world. However, as much as I still admire the lifestyle of China's rural farmers, I have seen many positive changes among the girls who have moved to Kunming to work with us. They become more inquisitive and confident. They learn to express themselves and start developing their own life goals.

I've experienced Aling's growth from Salvador's waitress to the accomplished artist and businesswoman she is now. I've watched Yaya and many other Salvador's mature into adults with their own dreams for the future. Kunming has given them the opportunity to look beyond their fate on the farm. It took coming to China for me to learn that cities are more than just consequences of growth. They are places where people can shed their rural shackles to become something more.

CHAPTER 25

UPROOTED

"Peas and fashionable meatballs," said the flight attendant over the plane's speakers. I wondered why they even tried to make announcements in English on flights when only veteran ears could tell that she had tried to say, "Please fasten your seatbelts." But I gave it little thought and just kept on sulking.

It was my fourth trip to Lincang in three months, and soon Lincang would be home to a new branch of Salvador's Coffee House.

Two of our best managers had recently left Salvador's to marry and move closer to their villages in Lincang. Late in 2012, one of them contacted me saying that there was a new development area opening up for rent in the city center, and they wanted to open up their own Salvador's.

Lincang is a small city similar to Xuanwei. Mining and tea industries had created massive wealth in the area and the city was growing fast. We had little doubt that under the management of our former employees, Salvador's could be successful in Lincang, but we were never too keen on the idea of opening more restaurants. After some convincing, I made an exploratory trip to scout out the space they were talking about.

The storefront was big – more than double the size of Kunming's Salvador's. Setting up a restaurant there would cost close to $80,000. That was money none of us had available, so after some consideration, we passed on the idea.

The Salvador's girls, however, did not want to let the opportunity go, and they told us that they wanted to invest. Eight Salvador's girls, along with their families, came up with nearly $40,000 to put toward the Lincang Salvador's. For us, it was shocking to see what they were willing to risk on such a venture. We came up with the rest of the investment to where the girls would own 48 percent of the new business. The eight girls who had invested were now our partners. They would take the risk with us, which to me seemed like a beautiful thing. If done right, it could work out well for everyone.

Three of our former managers, including Pingdi, decided to run the place together. They had learned everything necessary to run a restaurant, as each one of them had started out as a dishwasher and learned cooking, serving, ice cream-making, accounting, employee scheduling and even how to conduct employee meetings. They would be able to take care of the Lincang Salvador's with minimal stress and responsibility for us.

Soon after flying back to Kunming to sort things out, I returned with Kris and Wang Hu to start designing the space. We sketched out a floor plan with towering brick walls to be covered with a mosaic of shattered ceramic tiles. We built in concrete sofas that were shadowed by long glass lights on metal rails. And we were able to make space for a large kitchen like we always wished we had in Kunming.

After a month of concrete and metal work we were able to bring the Lincang Salvador's to life. We invited a number of local friends over to try out some select menu items. The girls in the kitchen were starting to wash and prepare vegetables when suddenly one of them came running out to find us saying that the water was not draining and had flooded the kitchen floor.

We called in a plumber who brought in his electric drain snake. After spending 15 minutes trying to pass the blockage, the plumber gave us a pitiful look. "I think your pipes go nowhere but straight down into the dirt," he said.

The plumber told us that because Lincang had developed so fast, these kinds of mistakes were unfortunately a normal occurrence. When the new building that Salvador's was in was constructed, only some of the plumbing was actually connected to the main line. The rest of the pipes went straight down into the dirt, meaning that all of the above-ground drainage we had built into the plumbing of the kitchen had nowhere to go.

It was a holiday, so there was no one available for hire to help us out. We had about five hours before our opening party, so Kris and I borrowed a pickaxe and a shovel and started digging. We dug down about two meters to go under the foundation of the 12-floor building where we could reach the end of the pipe. Just like the plumber had predicted, it went straight down into the dirt.

Back home in Colorado, this kind of error would have ended up as a lawsuit, but in Lincang there was nothing we could do but dig. We dug until our hands blistered to make a long deep trench all the way from the building's edge to the main drainage pipe. We busted the main concrete line open with a sledge hammer and poked through the PVC pipe. We got the water running just in time for our guests to arrive.

I was burned from welding and bruised from misplaced hammer swings. My hands were dried and cracked from concrete work. I was tired, worn out, feeling unappreciated and questioning what the hell I was still doing in China. To top it off, that week Steamboat Springs ski resort in Colorado had been hit with a record snowfall of 48 inches in three days. I was missing out on what would have been the best ski day of my life.

On the flight back to Kunming, images of 'fashionable meatballs' dancing around in my head, I started asking myself, "Why the hell am I still in China?"

I often think about how Aling and I could move to my brother's property in Costa Rica. We could run his farm and I could put more time into my writing. Or we could move back to Colorado. We'd always talked about opening a Chinese ethnic minority restaurant together. We could give Coloradans a real taste of rural China. But for Aling and me, China was still home and China was where our best opportunities were.

China awakened my inner entrepreneur. There are few other places in the world where Salvador's could exist. I wouldn't go as far as to say that it was impossible for me to open a successful business in Colorado or elsewhere, but it would cost much more and be far riskier. The amount of money we invested in Salvador's would hardly be enough to start a hot dog stand, let alone a successful restaurant.

I grew up with the idea that, regardless of class, the American Dream was available to everyone. But in America, I never felt the urge, or even the ability, to start my own business. Other than a lemonade stand, aluminum can collection and dog-walking ventures I pursued as a kid, starting my own business as an adult was never really on the table.

China offers the entrepreneur more room for new business ideas because many potential markets have yet to be filled. That is not to say that success comes automatically, and I think keeping Salvador's open has proven to be anything but easy, but the fact remains that China offers an environment that is more conducive to experimenting with entrepreneurship.

This is not only true for foreign investors. A number of our former employees have left Salvador's and opened their own businesses. Mengjuan, our first employee in Dali, left Salvador's in 2006 and moved around between jobs before eventually opening her own clothing store. Xiaojing, our original head manager in Kunming, opened a successful café of her own in Shanghai.

Zhuhong, our dreadlocked friend from Bangdong, had his own entrepreneurial vision to start a new business in his village. He organized 10 families in Bangdong to start Yunnan's first village collective coffee farm. The village invested in 100,000 plants with the ability to produce more than 20 tons of organic coffee beans, enough to make a substantial contribution to the economy of Bangdong.

Some of the businesses our friends started succeeded, and some failed, but just the fact that they could try is what makes China's business environment different from that of many parts of the world. The costs involved, the existing competition and the legal difficulties certainly would have made it too challenging for us to open a similar business in the US.

Early in our partnership, we tried to expand Salvador's with two small ice cream cafés. We chose locations that didn't work out too well, and we closed within six months of opening, but that is one major benefit of entrepreneurship in China – failing won't leave you broke.

For Josh, Naoko, Kris and me, Salvador's was only one of many different ideas we tossed around during our 10 years of doing business together. We had discussed opening a miniature golf course, a Mexican-themed restaurant, a steakhouse and even a boxing bar. In 2006, we spent two months working on a business plan for a $3 million ice cream factory. We were hoping to become China's first homemade ice cream brand, fending off the invasion of brands like Dreyers and Häagen-Dazs. We never followed through with the ice cream factory or any of the other plans, but we easily could have, and I'm confident we could have made any of them profitable.

In addition to Salvador's, we started an organic grocery store called Green Kunming, which was eventually incorporated into the restaurant. Green Kunming brought in more customers for Salvador's, and Salvador's customers often bought Green Kunming goods on their way out. And as people took notice of our desire to incorporate organic and healthy foods, they gained more confidence in the quality of Salvador's offerings.

Village Progress, our non-profit enterprise, was a venture aimed to promote the cooperation of business and social enterprise. A portion of all of Salvador's profits funded Village Progress art and health projects in village schools. The more our customers learned about our health and education projects in rural Yunnan, the more comfortable our customers were about spending their money at Salvador's. This led to a new idea.

One morning, I was flipping through my personal notebook. I skipped over the pages with the frozen yogurt franchise plan. I passed up the sketches I'd made for a new organic grocery store concept. I grumbled at the outlines I'd written for failed grant proposals. And I felt embarrassed when I saw the numerous unfinished book ideas I had on my to-do list. But when I landed on the page titled, 'Dali Bar,' I paused. Written across the bottom was a note to myself that simply stated, "You will make your first million dollars in two years." The note was written in jest, but it was also a reflection of the potential I thought Dali Bar had.

Convenience store shelves in China nearly all stock the same packaged selections. These include dried tofu, preserved eggs and pickled chicken feet alongside items more recognizable to foreigners like Snickers, Oreos, fried peanuts and crackers. There was a huge market gap for a healthy alternative to the typical processed snacks, and I thought that Dali Bar might just have that potential.

The day after reading the note I'd written to myself about future millions, I bought an assortment of dried fruits and nuts and asked the Salvador's girls to bake an extra batch of granola. We spent four months making different recipes, and the Salvador's customers bought them up as fast as we could make them.

One day we were approached by the owner of a Japanese-run factory near Kunming. He had gotten into the habit of packing Dali Bars for his weekend golf outings. He had some ideas for manufacturing them in quantity. This was good news for us, because if Dali Bar was going to have any real potential, we would need to find a licensed factory to produce them.

We designed the product using only all-natural ingredients with no added sugars or preservatives. We wanted to market Dali Bar as a socially responsible product with a portion of profits used to fund future Village Progress initiatives. Dali Bar would give customers a chance to play a role in social development just by purchasing the energy bars.

Dali Bar has the potential to grow into something even larger than Salvador's. We could reach customers beyond Kunming and throughout the country. There is no bigger market base in the world than China and we had the potential to be the native *Power Bar* or *Clif Bar* brand equivalent. We could market to students who didn't have time for a proper meal but still wanted to eat something healthier than instant noodles. We could market to the growing base of athletes who wanted a natural energy food. And we could further market to everyone else who just wanted a healthy snack.

It was China that made ventures like Dali Bar possible for people like us. I would never deny the fact that many have succeeded in the West in building up similar businesses, but even more have failed. It is China that has opened the door of entrepreneurship to us, and with the creation of the Lincang Salvador's, this door was now also opened to our employees.

CHAPTER 26

TAKING A LEAP

Yaya stepped out onto the edge of the platform, three stories off the ground. It was her turn to take the leap and reach for the bar hanging just out of reach in front of her. She was physically stronger than all of the other girls, but she was afraid. Her legs were shaking and she cried out, "I don't want to do it! I want to climb back down."

"You can do it," we all yelled back to her.

Yaya looked down at us and reluctantly inched her way closer to the precipice. Josh cradled his daughter, Miwa, while Naoko started putting on her harness. She was next in line to take the leap.

"You can do it," the rest of the Salvador's girls started chanting in unison.

Years earlier, when Yaya had only been working at Salvador's for less than a month, she had to leap over the bloody body of Li Yan to escape the smoke-filled kitchen. Amazingly, that wasn't enough to scare her away, and she stayed with us at Salvador's to become a trusted employee and a close friend.

During the first few days after she came to Kunming, no one thought she would last. She was shy, awkward and seemed to learn at a snail's pace. But with time she became a talented baker, then a personable and proficient waitress, and then an excellent chef. And after four years at Salvador's, Yaya earned a position as a manager.

Her parents lived on the hillside below their tea farm. The home was new, with clean white walls and a tiled kitchen, and it stood out from the other homes of the village. When Yaya had been younger she had dreamed of building her parents a new house, and so she saved as much as she could from her Salvador's salary to make that dream a reality.

Her parents were very grateful to have their daughter providing for them, but they worried about her future. The greatest desire of all village parents is that their daughter will one day find a husband and start a family of her own. But that was not Yaya's concern. She was independent and wanted to determine her own future. One day she very well might return to the village, and perhaps even marry; but if she did so it would be of her own choosing, not her parents.

As I watched Yaya high up on the platform above us, I couldn't help but feel proud of all that she had accomplished. I was proud to have been a part of her life. We all watched as she took a deep breath to temporarily settle her legs. If she could make the leap and hold on, she would be the first one to do so successfully, and would avoid the plunge to the ground below.

"You can do it, Yaya!" we all continued to chant.

She took two more quick breaths, bent her knees, then swung her arms. With all her strength she leapt for the bar. Her fingers reached just far enough to wrap around, but her momentum was too great and she couldn't hold on. She screamed and plummeted about five meters before the ropes arrested her fall and the instructors at the other end of the rope slowly lowered her to the ground. The rest of the girls gathered around Yaya once her feet touched down and gave her a big group hug. She was laughing and crying.

We all had to take a turn climbing the ladder, some more reluctant than others, and make our way to the edge of the high platform before leaping for the bar. But the bar was little more than a distraction, a point of focus. The accomplishment was in the leap itself. And Yaya, along with everyone else, succeeded.

We had closed the café for the day to partake in some team-building exercises that included a ropes course and water obstacles. Everything was focused around working together and tackling challenges as a team. After we had all taken our turns leaping for the bar, we were led to the last test of the day. We were told we had to find a way to get all of us over a three-meter wall. They gave us only two minutes to complete the task and told us we were not allowed to talk or make any noises while doing so.

After two failed attempts in which the course instructors scolded us for whispering and laughing, everything stopped being fun and became much more serious. Some of the girls even started crying. And to make matters worse, the workers at the obstacle course started shouting at us and blaring obnoxiously loud music. They were doing their best to both irritate us and create as much stress as possible.

On the third attempt to surmount the wall, Kris and the girls vaulted me up high to the platform, and I was able to pull myself up. Then they lifted up the tallest girl, whom I was able to help pull up over the wall. One after another we lifted each other until only two remained. The last girl had to lift the girl before her and then hold onto her legs as we pulled both of them up. Our arms were burning as we hurried to try to beat the two-minute countdown. We did so with 10 seconds to spare.

Suddenly the music changed to something soft and relaxing. The instructors, too, softened their tone. We gathered below the wall and everyone started weeping. We huddled together and the crying intensified. I started feeling the urge myself, and I could see Josh, Naoko and Kris tearing up too. We all stayed together in one big group hug until the crying died down into blubbering.

Although some of the girls were annoyed that the instructors had taken the game too far, we still celebrated our victory as a team. It was a small victory, but it showed all of us how important it was for us to work together, and how Salvador's had succeeded to build the unlikely team of outsiders.

Sometimes there are holes are in your life that you never notice until you start to fill them. For me, Salvador's filled that kind of void. And I think that to some extent, Salvador's did the same for our employees. As we taught them a little bit about running a business and living in the big city, they introduced us to a side of China that we would never have seen without them.

The girls left behind their families the same way that my partners and I had. Each one of us has been uprooted, leaping toward an unknown future. But together we forged a business, and more than that, we made a home. We encountered unlikely successes and endured unfortunate heartbreaks, but in taking the leap together, we all found a future together.

The happiest part of my daily routine is coming to work and seeing the lovely ladies of Salvador's. We've grown older together and the cultural distinctions that used to make us different have all broken down. We all care for each other like family.

Every city in China continues to fill with migrants from the countryside, and most cities are now comprised of more first-generation urbanites than native urbanites. It is the villagers that now dominate the cities, and they are the future of the country.

Due to the continuing migration, cities in China are growing at a rate never seen before anywhere else on the planet. China is in the process of building a new identity and these migrants will play a major role in determining the country's future economic, political and social maturation. As China is changed by those from the countryside, so too will the rest of the world. If China will ultimately be the world power that many prophesy, understanding the lives and dreams of Chinese like Yaya will be the only way to truly understand this country.

Living in China, I get to watch the country grow at breakneck speed, as in a fast-forward time lapse. It's amazing to sit back and watch how, even with extreme overpopulation, unabashed development, distressing resource depletion and constant social unrest, somehow the country functions.

China is full of surprises, and if there is only one lesson I can take out of living in China for more than a decade, it is that the unexpected, both the good and the bad, is what makes life interesting. I'm in China because I don't want routine. When routine is what I want, the Colorado mountains will still be there waiting for me.

For now I'll be content serving up ice cream and coffee alongside Yaya and the rest of us at Salvador's Coffee House, waiting for the next opportunity to present itself.

EXPLORE ASIA WITH BLACKSMITH BOOKS

From retailers around the world or from *www.blacksmithbooks.com*